NonProfit
NonMarketing

NonProfit NonMarketing

A Guide to Branding Beliefs and Benefits

Mark Mathis

Creative Director and Director of Cool at
ME&V Advertising + Consulting

To order additional copies of this book, contact:
Xlibris Corporation
1-888-795-4274
www.Xlibris.com
Orders@Xlibris.com
38091

CONTENTS

GUERRILLA MARKETING

ADVERTISING

INTERNET MARKETING

PUBLICATIONS

PUBLIC RELATIONS

For Liz.
See, I finished something.

Introduction

Why do nonprofit organizations need marketing? Marketing usually means there is some competition in the marketplace and requires a communications strategy to reach goals. For many people, the thought of a nonprofit competing is just too much against an organization's mission focus. For these people, a nonprofit should be about collaboration and cooperation. These are certainly lofty goals and, in a perfect world, make sense. But the world is changing, funding sources are changing, the marketing world is changing, and nonprofits will change with these new pressures and challenges—even for those who think they live in a perfect world.

But, let's address the concept of competition. I had a nonprofit board member tell me that the idea of competition is ludicrous within the nonprofit world. Naïve? Yes. Can't we all just get along? We can if you don't mind struggling for the rest of your career in a nonprofit. Every nonprofit competes every day.

- You compete for the best board members
- You compete for contributors' dollars
- You compete for grants
- You compete for foundation support
- You compete for good ideas
- You compete for state funding
- You compete for employees
- You compete for share of mind and relevance in your community

The last item is probably the most important. In your community there is only so much people can remember, recall or feel is worthy of their time and attention. And there are just too many messages competing for attention—from nonprofits and for-profits. People don't differentiate between non- and for-profit messages. The pervasive marketing noise is everywhere. So you're also competing against all businesses and organizations. Now go on the Web and you find yourself competing against everyone from nearly everywhere.

So you must market. You must compete. And you must succeed. Or, quit fooling yourself and close now. A board president I met said that her goal for the organization was to lead the organization to "grow up." Although she was talking about a wholesale maturing of the entire organization, I wholeheartedly agree that most nonprofits need to mature their marketing efforts.

Surprisingly, it doesn't take a lot of money to make your marketing more sophisticated. There is no difference between marketing for NIKE and any nonprofit. NIKE has more money to spend but that is a difference in scale and techniques not strategy. And since you don't have the millions of dollars NIKE has to spend on marketing you must make your money go farther. That means you need to be more consistent, more diligent and smarter about what you do. NIKE can afford to make some marketing mistakes. You can't.

This book is about successfully setting strategy and marketing for your nonprofit organization—although, quite frankly, these techniques would work for any organization.

As I started my research, I found a plethora of marketing books. Some spent too much time discussing theory. I couldn't finish any of these, but I did find them a cure to insomnia. Then others were based on the premise that everyone must be taught about the basics of marketing and advertising. When you read these Advertising 101 books you worry that the marketing world will completely change as you're reading the book. These books paint with such broad brushes that never do you get the fine details of how to put together a real plan—and then work that plan. Most of these books spend way too much time on placing media (television, billboards, radio, newspaper etc). This fills page after page of copy, but they don't tell you anything you can use. How about condensing all these chapters into one simple phrase? And that is hire professionals. Hire an advertising agency. We'll talk about why to use various media, but to do the placement, hire a professional. Don't spend another moment visiting with media salespeople.

This book does have many ideas that you can immediately implement. It also gives you a way to start the strategy process. It's easy to advertise. It's hard to set a strategy, prioritize goals and then develop a plan to reach those goals. Then, it is not only easy to advertise, but effective as well. Yes it is easy to advertise. There are hundreds of thousands of people selling all kinds of advertising from television to movie billboards, from bus bench boards to building wraps. Each salesperson has a great case on why you should buy their advertising. But your goal is an ultimate effect from the advertising, not the advertising itself.

It is not only time to grow up as an organization; it is time to grow up your marketing effort. And that means developing strategy. So thank you for buying this book. It will work if you put it into practice.

Your marketing is too important to just "wing it." It's time to think big, implement more strategy and begin "growing up" as a nonprofit organization.

Nonprofit Marketer's Inferiority Complex

L isten to how we talk in the *nonprofit* world: When someone asks you about where you work or what you do, do you tend to look down at your feet and shuffle a little and in the most diminutive terms explain your organization?

"I feel inadequate talking to our board members. They are so successful in business that they must look at us as unimportant," a human service worker once confided to me. After working with nearly one hundred nonprofit organizations and serving on many nonprofit boards, one thing I've noticed is that there is a pervasive inferiority complex among nearly all nonprofit workers. It's not often overt, even though it may be widespread; it is subtle, and it is definitely there.

Just as a tiny cancer cell can eventually envelop an entire body, this attitude of "smallness" can begin to overtake any successful forward inertia an organization has and becomes a debilitating momentum-killer.

Why would you define what you do by what you are not?

Part of the problem may stem from the word nonprofit. Actually it is more likely the prefix "non" that is causing most of the problem. In the Merriam-Webster Dictionary the prefix's first definition is: "not: reverse of: absence of . . ." However, the second definition is more telling: "having no importance." Somehow this "no importance" part of the definition is internalized by organizations using the nonprofit moniker, the feeling they have no importance as compared to the for-profit world.

One reason for this may be because we in the "for-profit" world take ourselves far too seriously. I'm always amazed by what we think is important. Board members arrive late at an important board meeting and announce how busy they are. I was on one board in which a surgeon announced that she had a patient on the table and just couldn't get away on time. We tend to give the impression that what goes on in a nonprofit is not as *momentous* as selling cars, selling real estate or reading contracts.

Helping troubled children, delivering food to the needy, or protecting battered women can't possibly have the same importance as making a business deal or suing someone or scheduling patients. The root of this difference can only be money. I've been told money doesn't buy happiness. I'm not so sure. What I do know is that money buys respect, status, expertise and the appearance of importance. That last part seems to make some people extremely happy.

Why was the prefix "non" added to profit to begin with? I don't define my business as a for-profit organization. My organization is defined by what it does—I work at a *marketing* company. Of course we want to make a profit. But I don't need to go around reminding everyone that profit is our goal. Why then would you introduce yourself as a nonprofit or, worse yet, a "501c3" nonprofit? Who in their right mind would let the IRS name your business category? Or, there is always the clunky comedy of introducing your organization as a *not-for-profit organization*? What would you think if I introduced my business as not-for-bankruptcy company? I suppose I could spend a lot to time explaining to people that we are a Limited Liability Company and the tax ramification, but it would get in the way of our message. So why then should you define yourself by something you are *not*? Isn't that a real negative way to say what or who you are? And can there be any pride in being a tax law category?

At first I consoled the person who was intimidated by the board of directors. Then I got mad. Why should you feel inadequate just because you provide one of the critical human services to society, or you work with the terminally ill, or because you raise money for kidney research? In fact, it is we in the *profit* world who should bow our heads in respect for what you do and accomplish everyday.

For some reason, those who live in the nonprofit world seem to think that in "the real world" or business world there is a knowledge base, skill level or operational techniques unavailable to the nonprofit service sector. Granted, in business there may be a more aggressive, entrepreneurial, cold-hearted, calculating approach to certain business issues and personnel matters. Yet the nonprofit world is just as dynamic, just as rewarding (in the things that really matter) and just as career-enhancing. It is important. In many ways, the marketing in the nonprofit world is more cutting-edge because it requires deeper creative thought, given the smaller marketing budgets.

The Calling

I haven't seen any research (but I've been told the Aspen Institute published many papers) to back up this next statement, but I've heard it enough that it must be true: most nonprofits attract people who have a "calling for the work." We are all glad you have heard and responded to that calling—otherwise there would be no one to provide the needed services that you so aptly provide.

Yet instead of the "calling" producing a strong sense of confidence, it seems to create a persistent sense of inadequacy or a tendency to self-diminishment. This, in turn, results in a detrimental effect on the entire organization. But "calling" itself results in a positive passion that is just not seen in money-making companies. Business managers love to talk about passion, but profit preempts passion at every step. Too many people redefine greediness as passion—their true underlying goals are all too obvious. People talk high-and-mightily about passion in the workplace, but it is a false sense of "fire in the belly." Counterfeit passion comes from self-importance. Real passion can come only from helping people in need. In other words, paraphrasing Scripture, the passion that profit companies worship is a false God.

Another way to look at it is this: for some, money is the bottom line. In nonprofits the mission is the bottom line.

So then, let's drop the name nonprofit from our vocabulary. For the rest of this book we will use "cause-driven," "mission-based" or "mission-driven" organizations. Yes, these terms are a little longer, but they better define the work and build the esteem of the professionals engaged in it.

Therefore, raise your head high, quit looking down at your shoes, stick out your chest and let the power of helping others fill you and give you a power-core from which you can draw to activate your organization. Be proud of who you are and what you do.

Why am I so concerned about your mental state and that of your organization? Because your attitude has an enormous impact on how you view and market your organization. There are hundreds of books dedicated to the power of positive thinking—and they work. We are not going to talk about positive thinking here. However we will be thinking and working a lot on visualization—and we are not going to think small.

How you see the future says a lot about who you are now and more importantly who you will become. If you are the CEO of your organization, how you see your organization says a lot about what your organization is and will be in the future.

What happens when someone feels as if they are not adequate? Mentally they shrink, and, physically, they look small as well. They tend to shrug shoulders, slump and make themselves as physically small as their mental picture of themselves.

Now taking the communications battlefield are a bunch of Type A, hard-charging spin-doctors wearing marketing armor and carrying swords cast of loud and literal words of metal. What happens when the Type As and the mission-driven workers meet? From our experience working with these organizations, we know the first words every *nonprofit* organization will speak: "Oh, we can't say that, we're a nonprofit organization," or, "We can't do that, we're a nonprofit organization," and, "That's good, but we can't, we can't, we can't."

All of these symptoms come down to one organizational disease—*smallitosis*. This is simply defined as small thinking. And small thinking leads to small acting. Small acting is followed by a tendency to celebrate small advances. Your vision statement comes off sounding like a *wishing statement*. Worse yet, no one quite knows what it means. The smaller you think, the larger your mission statement becomes. Your goal setting—if you do any at all—is limited to things you can easily achieve. You set the targets close. You begin to accept your fate as defined by others. You are experiencing the *"non"* effect. It doesn't happen overnight; it is insidiously slow and infiltrates every aspect of organizations who call themselves nonprofits. All too often it seems impossible to get out.

> *"If you're going to be thinking anyway,*
> *you might as well think big."*
> Donald Trump

That is really why this book exists: my goal is to give you some armor and weapons for the marketing fight. But this is also an attempt to change your thinking—whether you realize it or not you are in competition with other mission-driven organizations, other businesses, and governmental agencies.

Whether you like it or not, you are competing for money, attention, board members, revenue, and, for some of you, payments from the government. You're competing for grants, and just good old top-of-mind awareness. You need tools to successfully compete. And, just as in any battle, you must have the latest technology to win the day.

I Know: Let's Make Some Posters

I remember going to my first marketing board meeting of a county Red Cross organization. The meeting was scheduled to be about marketing. We were in a desperate situation. Money was very short, blood donations had fallen off and there were rumors that the organization was close to making layoffs or closing. I was working for an NBC affiliate at the time and accustomed to finding traditional and nontraditional ways to promote our programming and news to large audiences. I was not expecting what happened next in the meeting. After about an hour of throwing out ideas about how to generate some fast promotions, one person stopped the discussion and said, "I've got it. Let's make some posters and put them up in our business." To my astonishment, the committee loved the idea and before I could say "nonprofit," the issue was voted on. That was the *big* idea and the result of the meeting.

I'm not against posters, but 10 handmade works of art, displayed in 10 businesses would have the net impact of squeezing potatoes for juice.

Needless to say, I didn't make my poster; in fact I resigned the next day. Since then I've seen the same thing happen time and time again. Not always posters, but ideas the size of small posters. The same sentiment and the lack of clear strategy are always in attendance. Smallitosis attacks every meeting especially committee meetings.

Big ideas are not always big actions.

The real problem with the posters is that the marketing strategy was missing. There was no clear vision. No thought of what the impact of the posters would be. Certainly there was no accountability—what would the posters do and how would what the posters do be measured.

Board members, staff, contributors and friends of your organization probably love to talk tactics and hate strategy. Just for fun at your next board meeting suggest buying a billboard on a busy street in your community and ask for board suggestions. Watch the fireworks fly: "is that the right location, shouldn't we be on radio. I know a guy who sells bus bench boards, how about a larger, rotary board, I drive on the freeway and there are a lot of cars, should we be advertising at all?" Now ask what the billboard should say in five words or less and listen to the silence. Oh yes, some will try. But it will take them 100 words to tell you about the five words. Now ask the board what is the one message you want to convey; and what is the target audience?

Strategy requires discipline and total immersion in the problem or problems you are facing. For most, that is just too deep. Identifying even the slightest narrow audience category sends businesses of all kinds into a flurry of "we reach everyone" wishful thinking.

Strategy really means saying no. And that "no" is very hard to say. But it is the difference between professional marketing and amateur-hour. In other words businesses and mission-driven organizations lean toward the original amateur hour. It really is called focus; and when you focus on something everything else should go out of focus. The out-of-focus area is the *no* part.

To see the difference strategy can make listen to this story. The Coalition for Family and Children Services in Iowa was holding a legislative breakfast. There is nothing new about legislative breakfasts: stale pastries, coffee, juice and forced conversations. During the legislative session there is a breakfast, a lunch and an evening reception almost every day sponsored by some very needy organization or association. The Coalition wanted to give something to the legislators that would have maximum impact and help humanize their plight (over the last few years hundreds of thousands of dollars had been cut from state child welfare organizations). The problem was compounded by the fact that it was legally forbidden to give anything more than $2.00 in value to elected officials in Iowa. The big idea the Coalition came up with that had the necessary small price tag was to make sack lunches in bags decorated by children being helped by child welfare organizations. Children who were being treated by Coalition members had written very touching, hand-written notes to the legislators. Each bag included a note from a child. The lunches were peanut-butter and jelly sandwiches, an apple and chips. Each legislator—each skeptical and cynical legislator—melted when they looked in the bag. Many wrote notes of thanks back to the Coalition, with a note of thanks for the kids. Legislators who did not come down to the breakfast were delivered lunches on the senate and house floors.

You're probably thinking what's the difference between making posters and hand-made lunch bags? The marketing technique was hand-made just like the posters idea: however, the strategy is light years away in depth and positioning. The bags effectively reached the target audience head-on with dramatic effect. We reached our goal, hit our audience, and delivered the right message. Legislators are still talking about the lunches. The posters are in the landfill.

Nonprofits need marketing, not nonmarketing

For some reason, there is a notion that marketing or branding is not the same for mission-driven organizations as it is for other companies. Who says? To me, branding your organization and branding NIKE are no different. It is true that NIKE has millions to spend on advertising and you don't. However that's a difference in marketing techniques, not strategy. Strategy should never include the money. It is the tightly-focused goals and thinking of strategy that propel your organization to new heights.

The following ideas will help you think big, stretch your marketing muscle, and reach goals you probably thought were impossible. It's time to think big, plan big and execute big.

It's time to be big as well.

General Marketing

"Success in war depends upon the Golden Rule of war.
Speed. Simplicity. Boldness."
Patton's Field Notebook
Patton on Leadership

Visualize to Strategize

How should you start? The key to successful marketing is what I like to call *visualize to strategize*. You need to be able to visualize the future of your organization in order to really see the tactics and tools you'll need.

During the Winter Olympics you will see the downhill skiers doing their pre-race routine: eyes closed and hands out, they visually go through the course, every turn and hill, moving their hands with the mental terrain. This "seeing" the course helps skiers navigate an approximately two-mile course at breakneck speeds. The mental mapping of the course helps set the mind for instantaneous reflex response to the gates and course nuances.

You must create that same mental map for your organization. Sounds easy? It's not. All businesses and organizations struggle with visualization because it forces them to focus their efforts. Focusing means that one must prioritize—and more importantly, leave some things on the table.

For example, there is very cool restaurant in Cedar Rapids called the Flying Weenie. It sells Chicago-style hot dogs and has a plane on top of the restaurant. But the Flying Weenie also sells hamburgers. If a typical marketing committee of a nonprofit were to analyze the name it would probably suggest changing the name because it doesn't' reflect all the good food they sell. The Flying Weenie is successful in large part, due to its creative and catchy name. Does it matter that it doesn't say anything about hamburgers? No. In fact it would become less successful if it watered down its name. The focus is on the name and hotdogs. Both are great. Focus makes you great. Committees have a hard time focusing because everyone in the room is viewing issues with different focal lengths.

When I took a golf lesson the coach would have me take an easy, smooth practice swing and visualize the ball sailing through the air and landing on the green before I hit the ball. He wanted me to see the ball in the air and hold my follow through as I watched the imaginary ball land right next to the cup. It's partly the power of positive thinking and partly confidence-building. That is exactly what you need to do first: visualize your organization in five years.

As if the five years have passed, write down what your organization looks like. How many people are employed? Do you have an endowment? How much money are people making? What does the community think of you? What does the board look like? How do you deliver services? What kind of press coverage are you getting?

This is not creating a vision statement or mission statement. Most of these statements are useless in actual planning because they are too generic, too cliché-ridden and don't help you say no. This is an exercise meant to draw a picture of your organization for tomorrow. In fact you should be able to draw an actual picture because of your description. This is not dreaming, because the goal of visualization is to create a real, albeit perfect image of your organization—the ball sailing through the air and then landing on the green. It is this kind of thinking that will help you develop a marketing plan that will really be successful and move you and your organization forward. Hire some outside help to take you through this process, but don't do a SWOT (Strengths, Weaknesses, Opportunities, and Threats) analysis. Conduct what I like to call a visualization audit.

Conduct a Visualization Audit

"Nothing great was ever achieved without enthusiasm."
Ralph Waldo Emerson

To conduct a visualization audit you will need big thinkers from your organization. Leave the "that won't work" people at home. These are the same people who stayed loyal to England as our country was forming. They are nice people. When you're forming something new, you don't want them at the table. Many of the "that won't work" contingent don't see themselves that way, so you will need to be gentle.

You need big thinkers. I would strongly suggest that many of the people come from outside your organization to lead the charge. You need breakthrough thinking. Who better to not see the trees but keep a big eye on the forest than people who are not close to the organization?

So, don't hold the same-old SWOT analysis, don't rewrite your mission statement, don't rewrite the vision statements, don't hold a staff retreat, without addressing visualization.

24

Since I'm in the business, I can easily spot the sham visualization efforts. If you are just trying to lead your board and staff down the road of a capital campaign, you're not looking for breakthrough creative thinking. You're just looking for a quick affirmation of preconceived ideas about what will be good for your organization.

For example, I was once on the board of a national ethnic museum. I sat through a retreat where we analyzed the strengths of the organization. In the middle of this self congratulations about all that was good with the museum, an older gentleman suggested we build an outdoor ethnic café next to the museum. It didn't fit the process. It was too out of the box. It was too much for staff (one staff person barked him down with a statement that if he knew the state of the library facility he would not suggest that kind of effort). All I could think about was how Barnes & Noble was able to "eat the lunch" of public libraries. Libraries are stodgy, old repositories of antiquated ideas. Barnes & Nobles are noisy, fun, coffee-serving money makers—and, yes, some people just go there to read books and magazines. They broke the mold and now the mission-driven libraries are putting coffee shops inside.

Visualization allows for this kind of thinking. Just be careful who you invite. Staff should be part of the discussion, but usually they can only see the workload, not the opportunity. You want to see the ball sail toward the green, not the fact you don't own clubs.

Visualization Audit Workout Session

If you work in the service industry you've been to a lot of retreat sessions. They are all pretty much the same—and generate the same results year after year. I have facilitated many of these meetings and I'm always struck by how much power the facilitator has in directing the flow and adoption of ideas. Even subtle word changes as the meeting progresses makes changes to the scope and focus of the retreat. We are not trying to write some wordy mission statement or a strategic plan. We are trying to find what will make the perfect organization now and in the future. Visualization is a different approach that requires a different structure. We've all been to the sessions where a few dominate the discussion and seem to lead the group to one road or the other. The strong-willed can force their ideas, but this never leads to breakthrough creativity or thoughts.

Here is what seems to work best for this type of work session. It is built from creativity work-sessions and it makes sure all ideas are offered and heard by the group.

First, ask each question and then have people write down (working individually) as many ideas as they can in 5 minutes; then have people get in groups of two to three, sharing their ideas quickly and then beginning to brainstorm more ideas. Don't let these groups get any larger than two or three, because too many people will allow some of the people to slack off. The larger group will also defer to the person who seems to have the most knowledge about the organization. The small groups force even the shyest of people (especially new people to the board or other new people you've invited to your work session) to feel free to speak up and contribute.

At this point you are ready for presentations. Ask everyone to write out their great ideas on a sheet of paper that will be handed in at the end. But when they present, only let the group present their top two ideas. When you report back the results, list the top ideas as determined by the small groups and then all the ideas that were generated. That is the end of the first meeting. The goal was to generate as many ideas as possible.

The second meeting is a culling of the ideas, expanding on exciting areas and testing the ideas for validity. When you come out of this second meeting you should have a good description of the perfect organization (the perfect golf shot) against which to judge all future decisions.

The third meeting should be a prioritization of the ideas from the second meeting. This will be the least exciting of the meetings but no less important. This should be the final document that goes before the board as an approved visualization of the future of your organization. From this, committees need to be assigned and work-groups formed to make the visualization a reality. Visualizing your shot is important, but you still have to hit the ball.

Here are the questions you should explore to get to some breakthrough creative ideas and direction for your organization.

- What does your organization look like in five years?
- How is it different in five more years?
- Does everyone working in five years work for your organization today? What people have left and why?
- Are all the key managers still there? Why?
- Do you serve the same people in five and ten years? What groups would you add; who would you drop?
- What would Disney do if it bought your organization?
- What would General Electric do if it bought your organizations?
- If we are a success in the next five years, how will we know?
- In five years what will your stakeholders (donors and key community leaders) think about your organization?
- What will the community think about your organization in five years? How is it different from today?
- If you had to stop doing five things by next week what would they be?

- Are we the best organization in a five-state area? Why not? Who is and what do they do differently?
- List 10 things that must happen in the next five years to make your organization be successful and meet your goals.

All you need is a few sheets of paper to begin seeing your organization in the future. Then present your findings to the board. Tell them exactly what kind of organization they will be representing in five years. Assuming that many of your key board members might be in on the process, allow for some feedback and additions—but don't let *committee-think* kill the visualization. See the ball leave your club, sail high in the air and land on the green. See your organization soar.

Marketing Plans

*"Long-range planning does not deal with future decisions,
but with the future of present decisions."*
Peter F. Drucker

Marketing plans are a pain to write. Communications plans are even worse. I have written enough plans that the paper would weigh tons. Some are on the "island of misfit marketing plans." They are hoping some day to be used, but for some reason they are relegated to the shelf or closet. Others are living plans helping to propel companies to new heights of communication and marketing. Marketing plans are hard to write. I don't think there ever was a marketing plan job turned in at our agency that I didn't dread starting.

The real problem is that we all feel that we have a plan in our heads. We tell ourselves we just haven't had the time to get it on paper. The other problem is the cost. When you see what you are spending on marketing in the aggregate it really scares people.

We helped one college pull all its advertising together onto one spread sheet. The total was more than $200,000. The silence in the room after we did the final calculation was deafening. As each one in the room looked at the number we couldn't believe that all the little ads could be such a large total number.

Marketing plans are also hard to write because you must ask and answer tough questions about your organization. As you formulate your plan many good ideas, wonderful media and priorities are left on the cutting-room floor.

The Marketing Insane

I hear mission-driven organizations complain all the time that they are not known in the community; some even say that they are invisible in the community. I then follow with one simple question: "What is your communications plan?" That question is always followed with, "We don't have one. We don't do any communications." Well then, don't be surprised by the results—no plan, no visibility. No effort, no knowledge. No pain, no gain. Isn't the definition of insanity doing the same thing but expecting different results? If so, most nonprofits are marketing insane.

A marketing plan is a written document spelling out the goals, strategies and tactics needed to reach the planner's objectives.

The marketing planning process should explore any area where a stakeholder, audience member, donor or client comes in contact with your organization—from the front door to the back door, from how the phone is answered to direct mailings (fundraising, newsletters, board letters).

> *"The output of planning is not a plan;*
> *the output of planning is action."*
> MC Candler

A Complete Plan

Your marketing plan should begin with a goals page. You must know what you are trying to accomplish by your marketing efforts. These goals must be specific. If you can't write five simple goals, then stop this process and move to another chapter, because the rest of the plan will be a waste of time and effort.

Next, you should conduct a SPOT Analysis: This is a detailed listing of Strengths, Problems, Opportunities and Threats unique to your current situation. Invite key staff to a meeting and write all the ideas down. A facilitator can help with this process, but you can probably do this with key people from your organization and lunch.

Next, interview a few people from your target audiences and have them list a few ideas for each of the SPOT analysis areas. This will help broaden the scope and give you a more target audience focus from the start.

Marketing plans do not exist in a vacuum. Too many times the best laid plans fail because market conditions, internal capabilities, company history and on-the-street realities are not taken into consideration. The SPOT analysis is by no means a complete or scientific research project. It is purely qualitative in its scope and information. However this process can help build a filter from which all decision-making can pass to test idea viability.

After you have completed the SPOT analysis, break your marketing plan into these six key areas: Marketing Objectives, Marketing Strategy, Tactics, Timeline, Budget and Evaluation.

The Marketing Objectives are specific, attainable and *measurable* benchmarks for the plan. Where the overall goal is to move name awareness from 10 percent to 50 percent, the marketing objectives would be the smaller steps to achieving those goals. In this area you should also analyze and document the following:

- Identify and classify your target audience (or audiences)
- You should review all current media strategies and do a placement analysis (or effectiveness analysis)
- Evaluate your name and its appropriateness in the marketplace

The next area is the least fun part of a marketing plan. Everyone loves to talk about techniques and tactics, but few enjoy the strategy of the plan. You can see this in big businesses as well. Coca-Cola got so wrapped-up in its research and the process of rolling out a new product, they forgot to revisit their marketing strategy—that lead to New Coke, and that lead to near disaster.

The Marketing Strategy is the "game plan" through which objectives will be achieved. This includes a more detailed target-audience profile, integrated marketing communications strategies, and the "why" of the plan. In other words you begin to uncover the opportunities that might exist that you have not employed. For example, if increasing marketing knowledge about your organization, you would explore regular contact with a list of community VIPs or influencers in your area. Who are the VIPs and influencers? Where do they congregate? Who is in contact with them now? Why are they important to reaching your goal?

Next, are the tactics. To use our example, this area would include the "how" of the plan. You want to reach VIPs or influencers in your area, so one tactic might be to secure the list of chamber members from area towns, the member-lists from area country clubs, a listing of all politicians, and board members of other mission-driven organizations. Tactics should be the fun area of the plan. This is where the rubber meets road and your plan takes off. You will need a listing of specific tactics and costs of each.

As you write out your tactics, note the timing of each action item and the cost (estimate if you don't have bids). Then construct a simple budget and timeline implementation plan.

And finally the part everyone hates: how will you evaluate the results? You must have some way to do this devised or the plan is really an exercise in futility. You must know if you're successful. So, begin by writing down what you can do to know if the plan is a success. Conduct a survey of all stakeholders; hold an online survey; check inquiries on a Web page; review new contributions during the campaign; stand on a downtown street corner and ask people.

Benefits of a Formalized Marketing Plan

Still not convinced? Here is my last shot. Here are the key benefits to conducting a marketing plan process or hiring someone to write a marketing plan for you.

- It helps determine the best message and the best medium for delivery to each of your constituencies; and keeps you from buckling to pressure from media salespeople
- A marketing plan provides a new direction and new growth for your organization
- It helps determine the best way to gain support for your mission
- It gives tactical and specific strategies and allows you to utilize the strengths of integrated marketing
- It makes good use of resources; identifies needs in terms of staffing, avoids past mistakes and indicates where improvements may be needed
- It encourages clear and logical analysis of the problem or challenge and leads to its solution through defining each problem or challenge, setting of objectives and proposing solutions
- It provides a framework for viewing the problem/challenge objectively
- A marketing plan helps identify gaps in available information or weak links in the marketing chain
- It helps produce a more creative product
- It allows you to develop more effective marketing tools

Your marketing plan should take approximately two months to write. Any less time and you should wonder if you've put in enough due diligence to produce a thorough plan.

What's In a Name?

A l and Laura Ries in their book 22 Immutable Laws of Branding wrote, *"the most important branding decision you will ever make is what to name your product or service. Because in the long run a brand is nothing more than a name."*

Many mission-driven organizations spend little or no time developing a name. There is a real need to reassess your name, especially if you use the words *association* or *coalition* in your name.

Most names are developed quickly and for that reason, familiar words and names sound good. This familiarity happens in all levels of business because we tend to like the familiar and disregard the new. But, the new is where the greatest benefits are.

Above all, the most important function of a name is to be remembered. In "pre-cable" days, most people in television changed their names to short words that could be easily remember—King seemed to be popular. A popular weatherman changed his last name from Kronschnable to Kennedy. Today with so many more talking heads on television there is a real need to break out so you see names such as Solidad. However, some memorability is lost for the sake of uniqueness. "Unique," however can't begin to describe these mission-driven acronyms.

Try these on for size:

CADCA
Community Anti-Drug Coalition of America

NASSMC
The National Alliance of State Science and
Mathematic Coalition.
NCFSS
The National Coalition for Food Safe Schools

These names were established by committees trying to sound important or former government workers who have no need to worry about reality or raising real money. The names are an excellent example of how a word becomes familiar, so it then becomes overused. I don't know how many names contain the word coalition, but if you're tired of being an association it seems your only choice is a coalition.

Committees are so good at settling on the familiar (or cliché) because it is safe and everyone in the room can nod their heads in approval and feel part of the process, even when the process develops a name like The National Alliance of State Science and Mathematic Coalition.

Here is where businesses that need to sell something really break from mission-driven organizations. Where have you ever seen a business use a five-letter acronym for a name? You won't, because business names must really work. Nonprofit names must "make everyone happy." IBM works, but NAOIBM does not.

If the public can't remember your name (or acronym) then how will they look you up on the Internet, talk about you with other people, or write out a check to your organization? Great names mean something, but more importantly, they are easily remembered. What would e-Bay be if a committee of mission-driven people sat down to make up its name? The Coalition of Interacting People Selling Good Stuff to Help Improve Their Lives. The CIPSGSHIL or e-Bay?

If you ever travel to Cedar Rapids, Iowa, you must visit the Flying Weenie. It is a Chicago-style hot dog restaurant in Cedar Rapids. The Flying Weenie does little to no advertising, but its name is well-known in a 60-mile radius. The name is unique. It distinguishes itself from the competition. It is memorable. And the name does one more thing that many people forget a name should do. The name stands for *one thing*. Would it surprise you to find that the Flying Weenie sells hamburgers? Does it slight hamburgers because the word hamburger isn't in the name? What about French fries? They have been left out of the name. You cannot, and should not, try to say everything with a name. A common theme throughout this book is that if you stand for everything, you communicate nothing. In other words, if you predominantly work with children and families, you should pick one for your name (and I would strongly suggest children).

Some have said that a brand is nothing more than a name. So how does a six-letter acronym sell the brand? It doesn't. Just wait until we start talking about branding lines or tag lines.

Is it time to change your name?

For years, one fruit was the constant butt of jokes. Prunes just don't cut it as a hip sounding name for baby-boomers who are slightly constipated. Being regular is important, but without the right name prunes sit in the grocery stores. Prunes sound old and stodgy. No amount of marketing dollars can correct this misrepresentation.

So, the California Prune Board requested permission from the Food and Drug Administration to officially change the name prunes to "dried plums." The California Prune Board changed its name to the California Dried Plum Board.

Still don't think a name matters to your marketing? When you are shopping, ask yourself do you prefer to buy polyester or Microfibre® clothing. If you'd rather wear Microfiber® then rethink the name of your organization.

If and when you change your name there will be some down time when the new name will not be well known. This may cause a drop in contributions and some confusion in the general public as you begin to market the new name. However, you will gain a major public relations benefit from the name change. You must also budget some marketing funds to make sure that the glow from your press announcement continues to shine. You must not leave this to fate. Your newsletter, one press story, and talking to your board will do little to get the word out appropriately.

At the least, I would suggest billboards and direct mail to reach all your stakeholders.

From the day you decide to do a name change, it may take one to two years to complete the project. You'll need months in order to decide on a name, research the name to make sure it is not a registered trademark of another organization, research the Web URL and register the name. Then it may take several months to develop a rollout plan. And, finally, it may take a year to announce and rollout the plan.

This may seem like more trouble than it is worth, but think back to the Microfiber® example. Your new name will provide you with potential power that your old name never provided. If your name seems old and stodgy, don't wait for the winds of change trends to make you a "hot" organization.

It's Branding Kemosabe

I learned everything I know about branding by watching a television show as a kid. Remember this? "A fiery horse with the speed of light in a cloud of dust and a hearty hi-oh, silver."

"Return with us now to those thrilling days of yesteryear. Where out of the past come the thundering hoof beats of the great horse Silver (insert your own horse sounds) . . . the Lone Ranger rides again."

I loved that show, but it's uncanny how much marketing was going on in the weekly program.

First I learned that the Lone Ranger is not so alone after all. He had his faithful companion Tonto. "Yes kemosabe," Tonto would say. We all have a powerful, faithful, supportive Tonto in our lives.

Secondly, I learned how powerful a consistent message can be. Can you sing the Lone Ranger theme in your head? Most people think that the song is called the Lone Ranger song, not the William Tell Overture.

Then, I picked up on the fact that standing out in a crowd can give you a powerful identity. What did the Lone Ranger have that other cowboys didn't? He had a uniform—again, always consistent, always easily recognizable. But he also made sure that he was differentiated from the pack; he wore a mask. What a bold step. Only bad guys wore masks. Yet the Lone Ranger made it a positive, powerful icon. What about the horse? Was that a form of branding for this American icon? You bet, a beautiful white horse. He established strong color identification even on black-and-white TV sets. The bad guys all had brown horses.

He had a final *coup de gras*. I learned how to leave a mark with people. When the Lone Ranger wanted to leave his mark he left something highly identifiable with each person. He left a silver bullet.

The dumbest man in America was the guy who had watched the entire show unfold in which the masked man saved the day and, at the end, always asked, "Who was that masked man?" I guess you just can't over-brand anything. There still will be people who miss the message.

In my speeches on branding and marketing I give out a silver bullet to each person, when I can find the bullets. After 9-11, it is difficult to move 100 silver bullets through airport security. When I tell them that it is for a speech on branding I usually end up in a nice, gray room with a bright light in my face and two guys in black suits sweating me out. Of course the silver bullets are duds, just made for show.

This bullet is a symbol of how powerful a brand can be and how a powerful brand can leave a mark on everyone it comes in contact with.

Each day you communicate with people. Even when you don't say anything there is a perceived communications. Each day you leave your mark with people.

You must ask, "Am I leaving a *silver bullet* message with my customers and clients today, or am I leaving them something tarnished, old and, worst of all, cliché?"

Pavlov's dogs

Remember Ivan Pavlov? He won a Nobel Prize for his research into branding. Actually, they don't give a Nobel Prize for branding, but, if they did, Pavlov would have won it. Instead he won a Nobel Prize for his research with dogs.

Day after day Pavlov would ring a bell as he rubbed meat paste onto the tongue of a dog. The dog soon began to associate the taste of the meat with the sound of the bell until he would salivate, which became the dog's *conditioned response.*

It's called *implanting an associated memory*—and really, that is what branding is all about.

There are three keys: Consistency, he offered food with a bell, and the bell with food; Frequency, Pavlov did the technique day after day; and anchoring. You need an emotional anchor. In this case, Pavlov's branding campaign was *anchored* to the dog's love of the taste of meat.

It takes patience to do this experiment and to make a dog salivate. Now imagine how long and how much frequency and consistency it will take to *anchor* people to the message of an organization, especially since you don't have your audience in a controlled environment like a lab.

You may be saying, "Branding may work for products, but what does it have to do with my organization?" My question back to you would be, "Have you ever tried to raise money?" If you have, you know how important branding is. During capital-campaign feasibility study interviews you are really determining the value of the brand. It is at the moment when you ask what the level of support might be for this project that you learn the real dollar value of the brand. If the person doesn't know much about your organization (your brand), they will invest little or nothing at all. If they trust you, know you will do a good job with the gift, feel good about how the organization is managed and believe in the mission, then they have been branded to the extent of making a large gift. Time and again, it is the perception of the organization's brand that makes the difference in these large, organization-changing gifts.

So what is a brand? There have been stacks of books written on the subject. But I've found a short definition that sums up what I feel a brand is: "A position in the minds of your customers." In a sense it is like an "opinion" about a product or service.

That position or opinion can be positive or negative. For example, the Hardee's Paris Hilton ads (in spite of how appealing Paris Hilton is to me) showing her eating a giant hamburger on the top of car has a negative impact on me. I know there is little truth in some advertising, but I don't think the supermodel eats that much food in a week. I'm not the target audience for their brand, so it doesn't matter.

Typically, the brand is one or two words in the minds of your audience. I can hear the screams now, "All the time we spent on developing mission statements, vision statements, core competencies and value statements has been for naught?" Yes, at least in a branding sense. Brands, great brands, tend to lock into one word and smother it with messages that support that word. For example, Volvo stands for safe; Mercedes stands for prestige; Wal-mart stands for, well, cheap (but they are very good at it). What does your institution stand for? Can you define your organization's brand into one or two words?

Why is one word so important? It is simple, we live in a cluttered world. The word "clutter" was first used to define cable's over-cutting of movies with too many ads. A show with too many ads is cluttered with advertising. The problem is that today the clutter has grown in all media and everywhere you look. There are ads on the floor of grocery stores, in elevators, on monitors in cabs, and on the walls of urinals. Flat screens are everywhere. Billboards are now going digital so that you will see many ads, not just one when you drive by. Hundreds of channels now grace our TV sets; hundreds of radio channels are available on our satellite radio system.

Clutter is killing communications. It is estimated that we are exposed to more than 3,000 messages a day according to the book *Data Smog*. And that number will grow. Now add that fact to this one: the human mind can remember approximately 50,000 words. Today there are more than 1.5 million trademarks in the United States. That doesn't include all the non-trademarked names, tag lines, slogans and headlines. How much can you remember? One way is to understand your one-word brand identity.

Our marketing firm helped one organization work through this process. The organization is called Four Oaks. It works with children and families who have been referred by the department of human services in Iowa.

After a lot of thrashing about, we started with the "success guarantee" but then came up with the words "Expect Success." Our branding line is *success*. We want to make sure that once a child is referred to the organization, we will work with that child until adulthood to be successful. Unfortunately, the state will not pay for that kind of effort, but that is where the commitment comes into play. We are now working to make that a reality through investments, fundraising, and whatever innovations may come our way. Four Oaks "expects success" for all the children it serves. Do you see how that vision sets a course for the future? Finding the right one-word phrase has a way of focusing not only the marketing, but the entire organization as well. It is a battle cry for the future.

Finding the word is not easy. It takes long hours of writing. Here is a phrase to help you begin:

People support _____
(Your organization)
because it is the best at _____.
(What you do? Please notice the limited space)

And people will believe you're better than other organizations because
_____.
(This is the why question)

This is a good start. If you can fill out this simple statement you can begin to focus in on your word. You must be honest when you answer these questions. For example you must know your competition. Yes, you have competition. Who are they and how do you compete with them? Secondly, what is it that you do the best? If you can't answer that question, give up. Your organization needs to decide. You must have something that you do the best. What is it? It must be more than hope, more than a warm feeling in the heart. What is it that you do all day that really makes a difference?

If you find this process hard, then you are on the right track. Good writing requires good editing.

Benefit Selling

"Of all those arts in which the wise excel,
Nature's chief masterpiece is writing well."
John Sheffield
Essays on Poetry

S pec sheets, that's what most marketing efforts have become today. We cram all the information that we can into the space allowed whether it's an ad, one-sheet or brochure. This is because marketing is expensive.

Visually, this cram-it-all-in approach makes for a design explosion. There is no room for any white space, there usually is not a dominant image, and eye-flow (how a person looks from one part of the page to the next) is totally lost. What happens is that people get confused and look away or ignore the message. Besides the visual mess, the writing becomes a problem as well. Your copy and design need cleaning. Only a true experienced designer, not your niece or your friend's spouse, can bring discipline to your design. But your copy can be corrected today by subscribing to the principles of benefit selling.

Walk into any convenience store and look at the bottled-water section. The water in the bottle is free, available in any water fountain or faucet. The bottle probably costs around 5 to 10 cents. Yet we plunk down $1 to $2 per bottle. Why? It's the power of benefit selling.

Benefit selling is more than just a trendy marketing idea, it is a sales approach. Benefit selling addresses customer *needs* rather than the *attributes* of products or services. Attributes and features are merely characteristics of something. Benefits, on the other hand, refer to the *fulfillment* that an audience personally derives from a product or service. This can be a real or perceived fulfillment.

So let's take our bottled-water example. Water's attributes are that it's a clear, tasteless, odorless liquid that is shapeless, a certain temperature and named H_2O.

Now its benefits are what really sell this free product. It's pure, thirst quenching, refreshing, healthy, natural, cooling, restorative, and convenient (in a handy bottle). Because of the benefits you can see how this drives sales and the desirability of water.

Today, bottled-water is a $7.7 billion dollar industry. Sales of some bottled-water top other soft drinks. So, the next time you reach for some *natural spring* water think about the benefits and why you enjoy the water so much, enough to pay more than it is worth.

Benefits connect the customer to the product or service in a very personal way. That gives people real reasons to support a service or buy a product.

So how do you sell benefits in a nonprofit organization? The best way is to set up an attribute-benefit matrix. Here is a simple one we helped put together for Four Oaks Family and Children Services.

Mission Driven Organization
Attributes/Benefits Matrix

Attribute	Benefit to Clients
Nonprofit	We dollarize the value of your contributions by 10 times because we are tax-exempt, efficient and driven by a mission rather than profit.
501(C)3	Don't use this IRS government designation; there is no benefit other than the legal value for tax repercussions. Only use at the end of brochures so that the accountants know your organization has a tax ID number.
Charity	Charity sounds so needy. We want to have a need, but not be needy. How about using investment instead? There is a Return On Investment to your contribution that is measurable.
Donors	If you are a healthcare organization you may want to use contributors. Donors in healthcare give body parts. But being a donor is more than just a gift, it makes you part of the solution, part of the plan, part of the mission. You're more than a donor, you are a doer.
A gift	When you give, we give back tenfold. Unlike taxes, you get an incredible bang for your buck when making an investment in our organization.
Fill In the Blank	Take your attributes and put them in this matrix and make sure you are selling benefits rather than attributes.

Think of all the things you say about your organization. Are these sterile attributes or are the words powerful selling benefits. Benefits will always outsell attributes.

Speak Well

I'm not the world's best speaker. Yet I love to give speeches. I really have to work at it to make it look and sound natural. Now my wife, on the other hand, has a knack for giving great speeches. As a television news anchor, she does some 40 speeches a year, so you would think she would develop a knack. I've learned a lot watching her and others give speeches. In the mission-driven world you will be asked to make a lot of speeches, so you better prepare because you are not only representing yourself, but the entire organization and every person you serve.

So here are a few tips on better speaking to help you through the next moment in front of the crowd.

1) **Think Teleprompter.** Your speech notes should be typed in 30-point Times Roman typeface. The margin should be set at three inches wide and the text double-spaced. Use upper and lower case. Only broadcast anchors are accustomed to reading all upper-case text. There is a natural cadence to your speech; the tight margins will promote quick eye movement and natural breaks. If you find it hard to read your sentences, then they are too long and need to be edited. Spell out all numbers.

2) **Slow Down.** Most people read too fast. The maximum rate of speed you should reach is about 150 words per minute. This means each page, properly typed, should take less than one minute to deliver.

3) **Spell Out Words.** Spell out difficult words and proper names phonetically—use a phonetic system that has meaning to you. Also, write out all abbreviations with hyphens, PhD becomes P-H-D.

4) **Read Your Script Out Loud.** Surprisingly, most people do not read their scripts out loud prior to presenting to a group. When you read out loud, every time you stumble, stop or have difficulty getting through a sentence, it's time to edit. Reading copy out loud makes copy problems abundantly clear.

5) **The Power of One.** No matter how large the group, people are listening to you one at a time. They are internalizing what you say in a very personal way. When you refer to the large group it instantly depersonalizes your point. "For all of you here today I have outlined . . . ." Should be, "for you today I have outlined . . ." It's subtle, yet effective.

6) **Get a Theme.** I use the Lone Ranger as my theme for marketing speeches. So, I open with the Lone Ranger and relate the tale to my topic. The other key is to then end your speech with your theme. It will tie the speech together nicely. People will remember that your speech was nicely connected.

7) **Eye Contact.** "Look me in the eye and tell me that." We describe dishonest people as "shifty-eyed." So, look one person in the eye and say one phrase (rest on a person no more than five beats), then shift to another person. Go back to friendly faces throughout your speech for support and confidence.

8) **Lessons from Announcers.** It's hard to put excitement into your voice. People who make a living as announcers use these techniques to add excitement to their voice even though they are in a small recording booth: A) Every coach will tell you to stand on the balls of your feet to be prepared. It does the same thing as you speak. It will help lighten your step and make you bend your knees and get your body into the speech. B) Use your hands. Just the movement of your hands will help infuse inflection into your voice. It helps you to be dramatic. C) Smile. Smiling adds brightness to your voice, in sound and appearance. D) Pause for effect. Many speakers hurry through copy only pausing to change pages. Pause for effect, not for convenience. Look at the audience when you pause. The audience will hush.

9) **Plant a Question.** At the end of a speech there is always that uncomfortable time when you will ask for questions and then no hands go up. Sometimes you will get lucky and people will start asking questions right away, but why take the chance? Make sure there is a question, and that you know the answer.

10) **And Finally.** Don't make your audience conscious of passing time. "I have three minutes left" will drive your audience to concentrate on their watches rather than on what you have to say at the end of your speech. And finally, don't say "and finally." It does the same thing.

Humanize to Advertise

A lright, we are in the "human service" industry. So this next concept should not be difficult to grasp. But, alas, many marketing efforts today are glorified "spec sheets." The problem is that the goal of marketing is not only to *educate* but to *motivate* as well. To do that you need to appeal to the *human* benefits of any service.

Humanizing the advertising makes the connection and builds a relationship with your supporters. Conveying a sensory impression of your brand is paramount to success. Endowing your product or services with human characteristics is the best way to sell—it's a high-touch approach in a high-tech world. Humanizing connects people in an emotional way. In fact, there is research that indicates that when you see a person touched you respond positively, almost as if you had been touched yourself. It also seems to translate to marketing images. So we connect with the people that we see in advertising.

For years, the computer industry was mired in ads that only touted the raw muscle of a computer's processing power. The problem is that people didn't care how many horses it had; what they wanted to know was how it was going to solve real, human problems.

Advertising Age hit it on the head when it noted that Microsoft finally realized the sheer power of humanizing in today's hyper-market world.

"Microsoft continues to employ strong human images to help it sell something as faceless as software . . . 'Where do you want to go today?' campaign has allowed it to maintain dominance in the software field."

Humanizing concepts connect you in a personal way. According to Roper/Starch Worldwide, the most successful ads feature a person looking out from the page directly at the reader. Eye contact works in ads and in person.

So face facts, *humanizing your advertising* connects you to the audience in a personal way. It's the only way to build a relationship with your customers.

But the humanizing message goes far beyond pretty pictures of people in your marketing. It also speaks to how you write and express yourself in letters, brochures, Web sites and other collateral items.

Almost all advertising is viewed not in a group, but individually. Even in a theater, the ad is only speaking to one person at a time. You may have a group reaction such as a shared laugh or groan, but you internalize it alone. If it doesn't speak to you (because you're not the right demographic or psycho-graphic) then you tune it out. But the person next to you, the one with a ring through his nose may be tuning in.

Just by using the word "you" more often in your copy will force you to speak to one person at a time. Try to carry on a conversation, not a speech. Let the person know that you know who they are and how they think.

This is especially true in tag lines. I prefer the name branding lines because the tag line helps define the logo and name, something that the icon can't accomplish. It is not just putting the word "you" in the branding line. The focus must be on the individual as well. Branding lines must connect in the same way that visuals do on a page. Viewer benefit should determine every advertising decision on the page; the branding line should be directed at the reader so much so that the word you can be part of the line. You need to also remember that it is a tag line, not a brag line. My favorite branding line of all time is "You deserve a break today" at McDonalds. That line was used for more than 10 years. When McDonalds ended it, the restaurant lost some of its value.

Allen Hospital wanted to be known as the heart-care leader in its market. We wanted to focus on the patient. In the end we both won with a powerful branding line, but we staked a claim on some pretty valuable marketing ground as well. Allen Hospital. *The heart of your healthcare.* Branding lines really strike pay-dirt when they have a double meaning.

The following ad shows how humanizing comes together. Allen wanted an ad about its Level II Neonatal Intensive Care Nursery. The patients want healthy babies. See how we blended both and made some very compelling eye contact with the reader.

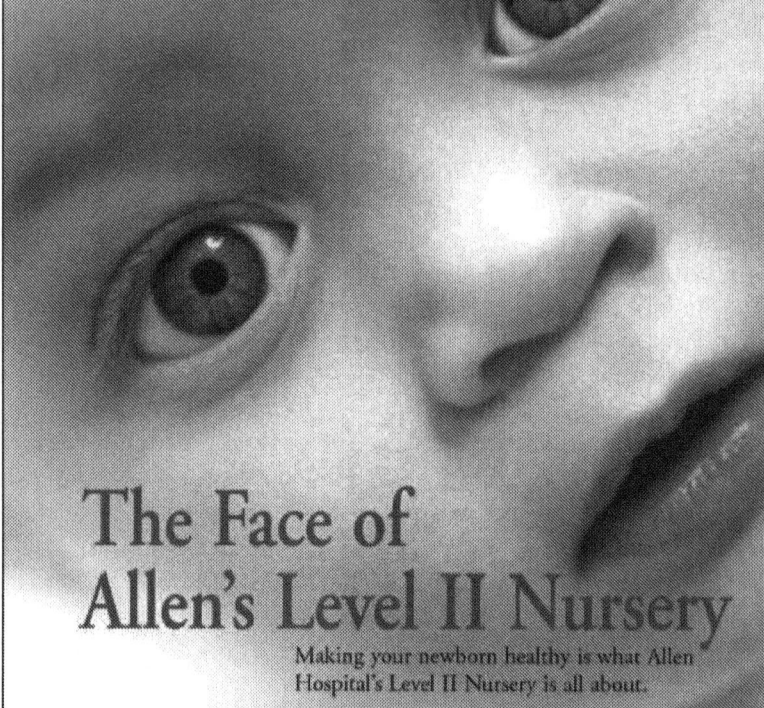

The Face of
Allen's Level II Nursery

Making your newborn healthy is what Allen
Hospital's Level II Nursery is all about.

Our Level II designation means Allen's staff is
specially trained to care for at-risk newborns
and mothers. So if you're faced with a high-risk
pregnancy, Allen Hospital is ready and waiting.

It's a service you hope you'll never have to use.
But if you do, you know you won't have to face
it alone.

**ALLEN
HOSPITAL**
The heart of your healthcare

www.allenhospital.org

Don't Hire Another Marketing Director

" I 'd like you to meet our new marketing director," says the beaming CEO of a mission-driven organization. My heart sinks, and the opportunity to do something truly effective falls with it.

"This is Heather, she is recent graduate of the University of Iowa in Journalism, and she is ready to help us market our organization."

Heather is paid $34,000 per year, with benefits its closer to $38,000 per year. She will need training and may attend a conference or two at $2,500 per year. She will need a computer, supplies, a phone, a color printer; let's say $4,000 total. That marketing director is now worth $44,500. However, the marketing director is in charge of a budget that is less than half her salary, and in some cases there is no budget at all.

This may be too broad a generalization, but I suspect it is true: Mission-driven CEO's love marketing directors, but hate to spend money on marketing. Why? Who knows? But it is one of the many reasons that organizations have little to no top-of-mind awareness. One marketing director just can't get out and meet enough people to make an impact.

Why not outsource the marketing? I know what you're saying to yourself, "the guy writing this book is from a marketing company, of course he advocates outsourcing." But let's look at what can happen in our example of Heather.

The Hazel Organization hires Heather after an extensive search (cost of time). Heather is 23. She has never negotiated media. She has never purchased printing. She has never made a speech. What she is, is she's cheap.

You assume that because you're a service organization that you can't do any better. You'll help teach her the job.

Now take the salary plus your modest marketing budget (if you have one at all). Heather was approximately $45,000 plus let's say, a $25,000 marketing budget. That equals $70,000. You talk with an agency that has media-buying expertise and software, designers, writers, Web experts and researchers. In the case of our firm you also have video and fundraising expertise. You will spend the $70,000 prudently: $20,000 on production; and $50,000 on placement. The key is that on media you are buying based on sound numbers, experience with pricing, reach and frequency information and people who can provide post-buy analysis. You get top-quality design and writing from people who know how to appeal to the emotions, not to the head.

It is true that you don't go to an ad agency to save money. You go to get solid marketing expertise and experience, plus ideas that breakthrough the clutter. That kind of strategy is not going to come from a recent graduate. A new grad, like Heather, doesn't have the experience.

So check your budget. Are you spending more on your people than on reaching your target audience? If you are, then reverse the situation immediately. It's time to be seen and heard, not build a staff.

In the case of the Cedar Rapids-Waterloo-Dubuque DMA (the television dominant market area) you could buy a reach of more than 90 percent of all people ages 25 to 54 with that budget. Also you would have an average frequency (number of times a person will see the message during the buy) of 9 times.

On the other hand, the marketing director could make about one speech per week with an average audience size of 50 people and only reach 2,600 people with a one-time frequency.

Evaluate your goals. If you want to get your message out to key constituents, spend the money on marketing, not on a marketing director. If you want someone to plan your parties, join other organizations, attend meetings, and wish for a real marketing budget, hire a marketing director.

This will not be a popular idea with marketing directors. Please don't get me wrong; many marketing directors do an excellent job for their organizations. The problem is when you have no budget; that is when it is hard to see the need for the human expense versus putting the money to use more directly.

Don't Tell Me, You're a Marketing Director?

Oops? You're a marketing director reading this book. Don't throw the book into the fire. I'm not against marketing directors at all. In fact, some marketing directors at mission-driven organizations are some of the best strategists I know. The key is what you do with your effort. Some believe being a marketing director is joining other organizations (Rotary, Kiwanis, etc) organizing events and putting up posters. This is not marketing. If it were, then why do people go years to college to get a degree in marketing? Marketing is judged by ROI, even in a mission-driven world. ROI is return on investment. What is the return on investment of joining a Rotary club? You can't be a speaker because you're a member, you can't solicit for your group during the meetings and you raise money for other organizations. Join Rotary for personal reasons: don't make your organization pay for it out of the marketing budget.

If you're a new marketing director, buy a book on marketing plans and write a complete plan for your organization. It should take you a couple of weeks to research and write this plan. Don't throw it together overnight. In that marketing plan should be clear goals of course, but also a budget area. Make sure your salary is included in that budget. At the end of the plan provide the ROI for all the money spent. If you can't clearly justify your position, look for another job within the organization to fulfill.

Color Marketing

When I speak to groups about marketing, I start with a slide of a John Deere tractor. John Deere tractors are made only a stone's throw from my Cedar Falls office. I only have the slide on the screen for one to two seconds and then ask, "What kind of tractor is that?" Never has there been a time when most of the room didn't shout, "John Deere." I then ask for a show of hands of all the farmers or those working in agriculture. Usually no one raises their hand. So how do people who don't farm or work in agriculture know what kind of tractor is on the screen? It is color identification. They know John Deere tractors because of their deep-green color.

Color is such a strong identifier for organizations and products yet few grasp the power. The reason is simple, because it takes incredible discipline to market with color.

Remember when we talked about the Lone Ranger and his horse Silver? The horse was a brilliant white. Everyone else's horse was brown or gray in color. But even in the black-and-white environment, the white color would shine through and even from a distance you knew the Lone Ranger was coming to save the day.

Color is becoming more and more important. Today we don't have Republicans and Democrats; we have red and blue states. When you feel blue you are down, if you're having a blue-bird day in Aspen it is a great day.

Many companies use color extremely well. UPS is brown; its trucks are brown, the clothing the delivery people wear is brown (down to the socks), the boxes are brown, and its message is brown ("what can brown do for you"). You know instantly when a UPS truck pulls up to your home. When DHL wanted to get into the shipping business they ran an ad with a photo on their truck. The ad said, "Yellow. It's the new brown." Without even mentioning the companies you knew who the DHL ad was talking about.

Target is probably the best at branding with color. All you need to do is walk into a Target store and the color and style are quickly apparent. Target even has a red song and all of the words are "red."

This kind of uniformity sends most designers screaming for cover. "How can you limit me so with one color?" they complain. Think of the color as a rule of the marketing game: just as Michael Jordan had to play by the rules but still found a way to be incredibly creative within them, your color is a rule. Find a way to be creative within it. One color, not multiple colors, can have a strong impact on your organization.

We worked with a small college client called Wartburg College. They asked me to address their staff at a meeting. One of the distinct benefits of attending Wartburg is the friendliness of the students and staff. Their colors are orange and black. One thing I know about the color orange is that it is a friendly color. It's the color of sunshine and orange juice, it's a happy color. In fact, Happy by Clinique comes in a orange box. So, I made some buttons with BE ORANGE on them and asked the staff to join me in the attitude of the color. When we then convened a group of administrators and staff to go through a branding-line creative meeting, one of the lines was Be Orange. Surprisingly to me, one of the administrators, Dave Ostrander, said that he was strongly in favor of Be Orange. It takes a lot of courage to promote a branding line that is so nontraditional for a college to have. Most colleges prefer something that makes them sound important, such as, "A Tradition of Excellence." Our marketing group (it was not a committee because committees kill good ideas) endorsed the concept and we completed a branding presentation to take to the Wartburg College president and board of directors. The sale was easy to this progressive, forward-looking board of directors. Soon we rolled out the Be Orange campaign to market to high-school kids. It wasn't long and orange began drifting into the entire college. In a marketing audit of the college we had discovered that the school colors were not being widely used and there was even some talk about changing those colors. The president stepped in and announced that orange and black would stay the colors and that Be Orange was the new battle cry for the college. One way to help enfranchise the color (although Be Orange means more than just the color) was with a one-minute marketing reminder during meetings. During monthly marketing meetings the director of marketing asked me to hold an Orange Minute with Mark. At these I helped draw attention to the color by showing how others are using orange and I brought an inexpensive orange gift as a tangible reminder. It has definitely helped orange become a white-hot color to the College and its friends. We found orange lip-balm, orange flashlights, orange tic-tacs, orange Jello jigglers, orange mouthwash, the list goes on and on. The message is clear; if all these companies can use orange, a college can use orange to its advantage as well.

Today, if you walk onto Wartburg's campus you will see signs in orange, banners that say Be Orange, students in orange shirts, and the track around the stadium is now orange. That is commitment to a color on a "Target corporation" scale. The college, staff and students understand the power of color-identification and color marketing. You might say that a college is easy to market with color. This would probably be right if only because colleges and universities have school colors for their sports teams. Look at college campuses today, however, and see how little color-branding happens outside of athletics. There are the few exceptions: Nebraska is Big Red everywhere. It takes a real effort to market a school's color. Now, if it is hard at a college or university, imagine how difficult it is at an organization.

When we do work for John Deere they send people over just to approve the green color on a television screen. Do you go to that length to make sure your color is right?

The American Heart Association launched the Go Red campaign. Now at events all across the country women wear red to show support and to let people know that heart disease kills more women than any other disease. You've also seen the popularity of the pink ribbon campaign for breast cancer. Neither of these campaigns would have had any impact without the color marketing and effort branding the cause. It is time for you to select a color for your organization and stick with it.

An Old-World
Marketing Technique

This is the oldest trick in the book, but it is one of the best. The technique is a testimonial. "Ta-Da."

We all know that word-of-mouth advertising is the most effective way to communicate. The problem is that it takes a lot of time to make word-of-mouth work. I'll describe a way to do word-of-mouth in a broader form.

Strong claims that you make about your services can come off as braggadocios. The reason is that, no matter how convincing, your claims are still unsubstantiated. Simply put, you have a vested interest. To fill your empty assertion with credibility requires a strong testimonial from a real and very satisfied customer.

But you need attribution for the testimonials to be effective. Make sure that you have a strong relationship with the person who is your testimonial. You may even need to find some form of remuneration to help solidify the relationship. When the testimonial hits, many people will come up to that person and tell them they saw the marketing piece. It is at that point that the testimonial will succeed or fail. If the person says, "thank you and I meant every word," you have a winner. If not, you have a problem.

It is also a good idea to have some kind of agreement letter between you and the person who is doing a testimonial. It is probably best for you to consult with your attorney to draft such a letter.

Testimonials are difficult to acquire. It seems like it would not be so hard, but to find someone with the right look, the right voice, and the right story takes a long time, not to mention they must be willing to share their story. Many will shy away from the limelight.

If you are going to the trouble of finding a set of effective testimonials, have a professional shoot the photographs. You will want to use these stories again and again, so find a photographer who can take great people-shots. I would recommend that you not shoot them in a studio, but in a setting that matches the story to give it more relevance. There are too many photo services that can provide people-shots for ads. The background should help identify the person as local. If there is not a strong visual for the background at your organization, try a background that is indigenous to your community such as a landmark city building or monument.

Differentiate or Die

J ack Trout in his book, *Tales from the Marketing Wars: Differentiate or Die*, states, *"To be different is to be not the same. To be unique is to be one of a kind. So you're looking for something that separates you from your competitors."*

Look at all the marketing in your community. Collect all the materials you can from as many mission-driven organizations as you can: brochures, fundraising appeals, annual reports, Web sites, logos. I think you will find that there is an eerie sameness to the service-industry sector.

If you cover up the logos, it is nearly impossible to discern which ads or Web sites are for which brand—if there is a brand apparent at all.

The sameness of look is caused by inbred marketing. Each business looks at its competitors' ads and designs just like the other guy. You feel comfortable with the materials when they look the same. But it is this comfort that is killing advertising and marketing. Just look at local car dealers' ads if you want to see an exercise in the *bland leading the bland*. Cut out the logos from a Sunday paper of car ads and you can't tell the difference from one dealer to another; then walk on the lots and you still can't tell a difference. That's because there is no clear differentiation from one dealer to the next. This happens in every category from healthcare to insurance to architects to dentists. Without a clear Unique Selling Proposition (USP) you will enter a world of the *bland leading the bland*.

However, every once in a while someone breaks the mold and says we need to stand out.

If you were an insurance company that sells supplemental health insurance through businesses you might have looked at all the current advertising and decided to go the conservative route, especially if you were a very conservative company. The television station I worked for was owned by the supplemental health insurance company, AFLAC. Knowing the company and its leadership, I would never have guessed what was going to happen next.

Dan Amos, AFLAC's CEO could have approved many other, safer ad concepts. In fact he had an ad with Ray Romano and children in a playroom with building blocks that then spelled out AFLAC. It was a very sweet concept.

The Ray Romano ad was tested and it did very well. And then a duck quacking AFLAC was tested. The tests showed the duck pulled better, but what would you have done? Would you have selected the conservative, safe, cute ad with the Everybody Loves Raymond star? Or would you choose the risky, break-out ad featuring a duck? I have sat in many creative presentations and, 9.8 out of 10 times people are too afraid to try something outside (or just on top of) the box.

When the promotion managers from the other AFLAC stations would get together we always thought the name sounded like a cat coughing up a hair ball (now, that would have been out there) but, luckily, Mr. Amos decided to go with the duck.

I was speaking to a college group of about 30 students. I asked who knew about AFLAC. They all raised their hands and one student quacked. Now, that is powerful considering none of these students are in need of the company's products. So they are out of the target market. Just the same, the students' recognition is not surprising. AFLAC's name recognition in the US climbed from 2 percent in 1990 to 90 percent today. Sales jumped as well. Can you name another company in the supplemental health insurance industry? I doubt it. That's the power of breakthrough advertising. The AFLAC advertising is a clutter-buster as well as a category-buster.

What can you learn from this? You need to stretch your message and stand out from the crowd. You don't need a funny campaign or a duck. What you need to do is differentiate yourself from the others marketing similar services.

Stop Copying

I s nonprofit Latin for copying? I've never experienced so much blatant copying of ideas, concepts, projects or events. CASE, the Council for Advancement and Support of Education, gives awards and holds educational programs for higher education all over the country. However, the ongoing joke is that their acronym stands for Copy And Steal Everything. If you attend a CASE awards program you will see next year's entries; just look at this year's winners. If students did this they would receive an "F." Marketing directors at colleges copy too, but they are rewarded. I think it is called "best practices."

It is true that we all copy ideas and themes to some extent in the marketing world. In the mission-driven arena copying occurs too, though it seems without any thought to the strategic implications of doing so.

At no time was this more apparent than after the wildly successful "Got Milk?" campaign launched by the California Milk Board. The California Milk Board didn't want to focus on the health benefits of milk as other milk groups had done. It wanted something different. For those of you who would like to say "that's so negative, we can't use that," "got milk?" is a negative campaign. It says you don't have milk at the critical moment when you need it. The agency called the campaign "the deprivation strategy" because the ads focused on the absence of milk.

The campaign won national awards and acclaim. So what's a nonprofit to do? Got ideas? No? Then copy. The "Got _____?"(fill in the blank) idea was formed. Even in our little state of Iowa the University of Iowa athletic department thought the campaign was so good they first used it for men's basketball and then for women's basketball. "Boy, that makes me jump up and buy tickets." Hawkeye Community College thought it was so good that they used it for student recruitment with "Got Class?" Then the Meskwaki Indians thought it was so good they started the "Got Cash?" campaign. Now local hospitals have "Got Heart?" ads.

What might even be more unfortunate is that these groups thought their idea was so good they may have even entered it for an awards campaign. Unfortunately, this is copying without understanding. The strategy behind it is dangerous, because, for the most part, the advertising is wasted.

So, the next time you want to copy someone, copy the execution but not the message. The message, especially a national message, is designed and tested to reach a particular audience. When you use it on a local campaign this only shows your cavalier approach to your messaging to your key stakeholders. It's little-thinking, and it doesn't work.

What Would Disney Do?

You don't need high-priced marketing help. You can brand your organization like no other by conducting a Disney retreat. Disney may be for kids or the kid in all of us, but don't be fooled, they have no Mickey Mouse marketing operation.

Disney is the undisputed king of marketing, to kids of course, but also to adults. Why else would adults spend way too much money ($12 hamburgers), stand in long lines, get kids up at the crack of dawn and then keep the kids up until after 10 pm, buy ponchos for the ten-minute daily rain, buy Mickey ears that will not be worn again, spend even more money, and then go home and start planning the next trip.

When you have your retreat you only need to ask one question, "If Disney bought your (camp, museum, church) what would they change to 'Disney-fy' the operation?" At a meeting of church camps we found some really interesting ideas. Church camps across America are struggling to compete with soccer and increased summer-sports activities. Parents know they can only get sports scholarships by pushing their kids all year. Campers seek technology (why spend a week without computers, video games, cell phones or iPods) and academic opportunities (spend a week in the woods or at a science week at a college).

As we talked some ideas started to percolate about creating the Disney-fied Church Camp:

■ Disney would build condos on valuable land so that people could retire to the camp and then the retirees would become an excellent source of cast members (Disney calls employees cast members because they are always on stage, however I don't know what Disney calls volunteers).

- Disney would take the revenue from the condo sales and build some feature events at the camp. They'd build the longest zip line in the state, the largest rock-climbing wall, an indoor water-park, paint-ball fields and/or a kayak course. Whatever Disney built would be big, exciting to kids and it would be newsworthy throughout the region. Disney would make sure the camp had something that would give the camp incredible talk-value to kids of all ages.

- Disney would put a better "face" on the camp. They would include a better sign coming off the main highway and at the entrance to the camp. The camp itself would be better marked so that people would feel comfortable even on the first day.

- Disney would sell more to kids. Most camps limit purchases during camp, so most kids go home with money. I'm sorry for the moralist of the group, but Disney would view that as money on the table. (Please don't whine that you don't have money to compete if you won't bring in the revenue.) Each major accomplishment would have its own items to buy. The Monster Zip (the largest zip line in the region) would have a shirt that says "I rode the Monster at OrgX Camp" and a small *www.OrgXCamp.org* would adorn the shirt as well. There would be a key-chain carabiner for the rock climbing wall and little horses with the name on them that represent the horse the kid rode. The store would be open all day, every day. Disney would research what kids want in a store and would let kids make the decision, not an adult. Think about your store. In museums, why are the stores relegated to a corner of a separate room? This arrangement means you have to staff two areas, the store and the ticket areas. Put the store out front so that people coming into the museum and going out of the museum must pass through it. After many Disney rides, customers walk through a Disney store with items that relate to the ride they just completed. It is pure marketing genius.

- Disney would create some proprietary music and enfranchise it into the culture. Campers would be able to download songs (for a price) from the Web site so that the kids would know all the songs before they get to camp. They could also download a pod-cast that shows all the movements that go with the songs.

- Disney would make stars of the staff on the Web site to help pre-sell the experience and build excitement for the week.

- Disney camp would make sure that the first few minutes people are on the grounds would be exceptional for kids and the parents. At a YMCA camp that I take my daughter to, we have to wait in a long line in the sun to get to her cabin. Disney would send out their costumed characters. The YMCA camp should send out the guitar players and a little refreshment. It would start everyone's week on a great note.

■ Disney would fundraise at every possible point. When campers are done with the week, many have money left in their accounts. Most camps just send the money back. Why not ask the parents to make a contribution? The only cost is a card or letter to the parents. You can even ask right when the parents are setting up the account. Disney would send letters out immediately asking if parents of kids in a particular cabin would help support renovating the area so that it is a better experience for all campers next year.

■ Disney would not fight soccer camp, computer camp, and educational camp. It would embrace those and make them even better. Theme camps would teach kids how to make videos and their own podcasts. They'd bring in a soccer star to run drills. They would have science, math and writing part of the camp experience for those who want it (all for a fee). And Disney would embrace technology: they would use e-mail, instant messaging and text messaging to reach kids and talk to them all year about the camp experience.

■ Disney would find a way to make more per camper by offering early registration and guaranteed cabin pairings for a fee. Most camps do it now, but it seems like more of an effort for staff to keep it organized. Let people spend more to guarantee weeks rather than trying to be "fair." Fair is not bringing in enough to keep the camps going.

Are you getting the picture? Disney is really about thinking out of the box and finding new ways to reach goals. Most camps bristle, especially the church affiliated camps, at the idea of such commercialization. At the same time they find themselves in competition with other organizations and inching toward irrelevancy. Some face bankruptcy.

Board of Directors

"You can be a board member; you can be on the board of directors; but when you become a 'board of partners' then and only then do you really begin to make good happen."
MC Candler

Board of Directors

There is no other group that you need to keep as informed and involved in your organization. However, the board is also your most powerful *buzz marketing* group you have in the community.

Board members tend to be involved with many groups and organizations; their ability to spread the right message is really unsurpassed. Not even your employees have the board's macro view of your organization. Board members also tend to circulate in the kinds of circles you want your organization to be in.

Board members have a large drawback; they usually don't know the organization well enough to speak on its behalf when they are not in the presence of a staff member. Some of this comes down simply to training. And that should be a focus of your board meetings and retreats. Another component is having the right marketing tools.

Business Cards for Board Members

Being a board member is pretty much a thankless job. Maybe you get an occasional photo in the paper or you appear in a newsletter, but for the most part you remain somewhat anonymous.

Many board members also participate in lobbying efforts on behalf of cause-driven organizations. These usually include an event or function at the statehouse where they mix and mingle with legislators and lobby for your cause.

The problem is that most of the legislators can't remember your names or who the organization's visitors are representing. If your group is hosting the event it is usually not a problem. However, if you are co-hosting an event, or if you're part of a coalition of people, your message may get lost in the shuffle.

For Four Oaks, we made board-member business cards just for these occasions. The card simply lists the name and address and the fact the person is a board member for Four Oaks. It could have included a company name, but I would suggest leaving that up to the individual board member.

The best part about the card, for my part, is it gave me an opportunity to break the ice with legislators. The legislators were taken with the card and many wrote a note on the back of the card as I circulated through the room.

If you are discussing a more complicated issue, you may want to give board members a talking point card that includes some of the information you want to make sure is disseminated to legislators. This can be done by making the business card a fold over card and this will give you another two panels on which to include information.

Here are a few ideas to help your board help you market the organization.

- Talking points. Provide board members with 3 X 5 inch cards with three to four key talking points for them on key issues facing the organization.
- Elevator speech. This name is really a definition of how long a speech should be about an organization: about as long as an elevator travels one to two floors. For example, I'm an Org X board member; we do blah, blah, blah, blah, blah. You want a speech only to cover a few floors, no longer than a one- to two-minute description of the organization and how it benefits the community and the people it serves. The elevator speech is a very important piece of communications because word-of-mouth advertising (the most effective advertising) occurs every time the board member is asked about your organization at a party, work, events or at one-on-one meetings. The elevator speech needs to have plenty of benefits, but also pull at the heartstrings. A simple story can do that, but make sure to keep the speech as short as possible.
- Board member recognition. In the offices and homes of board members you have an opportunity to market to an influential audience. Be very careful what you select as an item. It needs to be prestigious enough so that people will want to display it. Most board members have many plaques. A 3.5 inch square wooden stand with a glass-cut object and a nameplate that states Org X board member is enough of a conversation-starter. When you present board members with this item, make sure they understand the marketing implication.

Don't skimp. These need to be fine enough for the board member to be proud enough to display them, and handsome enough to elicit questions from office visitors.

- Past board member recognition. Most board members are thanked when they come off the board. But a well-placed plaque or object that recognizes the board member will be an excellent way to market in the offices and homes of former board members for years to come. Some may not hang them up or display these thank-you gestures but, for those who do, it may be a powerful conversation-starter. Again, don't skimp on the item. Think of it as buying space in a very expensive medium.
- Newspaper announcements. Many local papers will carry a photograph and brief description of new board members or board members elected to officer positions. Instead of sending these announcements together in batches, send one per week to keep your organization's name in the paper for as long as you can.
- Commitment for letters. When you do your board orientation, tell board members that you would like them to write two to four letters to the editor each year. You can provide copy from which the board member can write the letter, but by getting the expectation up front there are no questions later when you really need the support. Letters to the editor are free marketing for your organization. You should try to be in the paper once per month. Also ask for a commitment from the board member to write one letter a year to state legislators. This will probably be dictated by what legislation is coming up, but even a letter thanking the legislators for support throughout the year will be helpful in future efforts.

Events

Event Marketing

One of the best ways to fundraise and friendraise is to hold an event. There are hundreds of event ideas. The problem is that there are so many events by so many organizations that it is difficult to hold something that will be meaningful and attract a large audience.

Even though you hold an event, don't think it will do what you want. An event is a communications vehicle, it tells people a lot about your organization. Unfortunately most events are major "anticipointments." There is usually a great deal of hype, colorful invitations, and anticipation. But many end up being low on delivering a real memorable evening or event and some are just disappointments. And that is an anticipointment.

Two events were held in Des Moines on the same night: one was a dinner, auction and dance; the other was a wine tasting. Both were first-time events. The typical dinner-auction-dance attracted less than 100 people; the wine tasting drew 600 people.

Both were fundraising events, but the wine tasting offered a true experience and value to the attendees. The *tired* dinner-auction-dance offered the usual bland fare. Which event do you think raised the most money? The wine tasting hit the jackpot.

Let's take a lesson from stores. As stores compete with the convenience, selection and low prices on the Internet, the smart stores are focusing their effort on making the shopping trip an experience. Just walk into a Barnes & Noble and then walk into your public library. You notice the difference immediately. The experience in one is warm, inviting with a vibrancy of new ideas. The library feels like a dinosaur ready to walk into the sunset.

Events tend to be copies of other events. A golf event is a success for one organization, so everyone thinks, "let's have a golf event and then we can raise a lot of money."

Events must become very special or they run the same risk as stores not paying attention to the high tide of progress.

Start With the Audience

Most events start with a flawed premise—form a committee, get people together and then raise money. However, many events just break even and then the results are, "we raised a lot of friends."

Let's start with a different concept. How about setting fundraising goals and then determine the best way to raise that money. If it is an event, then the important question is, "who do we want to invite and what kind of event would they enjoy." In other words, start from the audience and work backwards. What would really be on target is to do some research with this group to find out what would really make a difference.

So, have you heard of this kind of thinking? "Let's have an auction and a nice dinner, we'll hold it at the country club, we will get people to donate items, and then have a silent auction and a regular auction for other items." First, the kind of people you usually want to attract are the people who are wealthy enough to belong to the country club so that is not special. Most donated items are things stores can't sell and the effort to collect all of those items could have gone into a mini-campaign that could have raised much more money without the event.

Here's a different premise. Who are we inviting and what event would they like to attend? Now that is a different focus. This form should help you ask and answer the critical and strategic questions before you go down the event road.

1) Why do you want to have an event? If it is to friendraise, don't combine it with fundraising. Friendraising is so much more effective when it is done in small intimate groups and connected directly to your organization.

     _____

     _____

     _____

     _____

2) How much money do you want to raise? Most events don't have a real budget. You need a number: $15,000; $50,000; $100,000. And it should be a net number.

_____
_____
_____
_____

3) What is the best way to raise this money? You must be truly honest. A golf outing that costs you thousands of dollars in volunteer and staff hours and only raises $15,000 is a flop—I don't care how many friends you raise. Plus, the chance of spending more than you make with that small of a goal is a strong possibility. For example, what if it rains or is cold and few actually attend?

_____
_____
_____
_____

4) Who do you want to attend? And the answer can't be "rich" people. Who do you really want? People who will buy $100, $500, $1,000, $2,000 or $3,000 of merchandise? Wouldn't you be better off approaching these people directly instead of inviting them to an event?

_____
_____
_____
_____

5) How many people will attend? Set a number. You can't budget if you don't set a realistic goal. Too many people may make your event seem non-exclusive, too few, a flop.

_____
_____
_____
_____

6) Now, divide the people by the total you want to raise. If you want $50,000 and you estimate 200 will attend, that is $250 per person. Now add potential expenses to the total: dinner, entertainment, marketing, staff time (yes, staff time is a real cost of sales). Let's say another $50 per person. So now you need 200 people who will spend $300 each. That is a realistic number. Now think, who can afford for an event like this at $300 per person? Probably not anyone with a household income of less than $100,000 ($300 is 7% of the monthly take-home

pay for a $100K household). Check you local statistics and see how many households meet that criteria.

_____
_____
_____
_____

7) What kinds of events in your community attract that kind of money and that kind of audience? If there are some mission-based organizations making that kind of income list those, but think of the other public or private events that reach a high-spending level.

_____
_____
_____
_____

8) What are the kinds of things that money (normally) can't buy? For example, front row seats at Easter services, front-row seats at kids music events, being CEO of a major company for a day or Mayor for a day, flipping the coin at a major college game, a local chef cooks in your home, a private driver for a week, seats to watch a popular band warm up, etc.

_____
_____
_____
_____

9) What are the kinds of things this audience would like to learn about? They must be unique, exclusive, and if a little dangerous, that can help as well. Here you must really use your research capabilities. Check popular magazines such as People, Business Week and USA Today, for trends, celebrities and ideas. Select fine wines. Avoid the cheap stuff. Remember, the guests have to spend $300 per person and these kinds of people know about Silver Oak, Opus, Caymus and Stags Leap. A-list earning opportunities might include: rolling cigars, making a perfect martini, gourmet food preparation, NASCAR simulators, shooting machine-guns, producing and editing their own videos on a computer. Bring in a star or business celebrity. Don't throw out any idea solely for cost at this point. If you could bring in a star for $10,000, that might be just the ticket to charge $200 per head and you'd be on your way to the total needed.

_____

_____

_____

_____

10) What would make your event a must-attend? For example, an event that sells out because you limited the tickets is the best way to give your event prestigious status.

_____

_____

_____

_____

Events Never Sounded So Good

W hat is the most important part of an event that never seems to go right? It is the sound system. It is often times critical to the success or failure of an event, yet few committees, organizers, speakers or board members give the sound-system a second thought until disaster strikes.

Spend the money on expertise and adequate speakers to make a great-sounding event. The acoustics of most large halls are poor; often times they are echo chambers that amplify the talk of drink-plied donors and friends of your organization.

Auctions become unbearable with poor audio. It is necessary for people to hear descriptions of the items, yet as the drinks flow it becomes impossible to hear over the individual discussions. Yelling for quiet only hinders bidding. You want a fun atmosphere which means people will talk and enjoy themselves at your event. The key is to be able to manage the situation with adequate and controllable amplification.

Don't rely on the hotel or convention center room's audio system no matter what people tell you. You need an independent system with a speaker for each of the corners: so for most of you that means a minimum of four speakers. You must have speakers at the back of the room to hit those who are least likely to listen and most likely to talk.

For microphones, wireless are best so the hosts can circulate, but make sure there is one microphone hard-wired and at a podium.

I highly recommend that you hire a company to do set up, monitor the sound during the program and then take the sound system down. A band or music system is not appropriate. Band people are interested only in the musical sound, not in being understood. Have you ever listened to a band where you couldn't understand the words? Also, band members are unreliable when it comes to making sure that you have volume when you need it.

My wife and I have hosted many events in all kinds of homes, hotels and rooms. Invariably, the sound system gives out at the most inopportune time. Committees have spent hundreds or thousands of hours planning the event only to have a cheap sound system ruin the occasion.

If you want to sound like a winner, you have to have the right equipment. And then conduct a real sound-check to make sure all can hear. Remember that in an empty room sound carries. A room that is full of people muffles the sound because of all the bodies and clothing, not to mention the competition from all the chatter. So, make your information heard loud and clear, and make sure your event sounds great.

Golf Events

"Eighteen holes of match or medal play will teach you more about your
foe than will 18 years of dealing with him across a desk.
Grantland Rice

" I could golf every week," said one exasperated business owner. The ubiquitous golf outing was once a wonderful escape from work on the behalf of a good cause. It has now become drudgery. Some are well-run events that people look forward to every year, and others desperately need to go back to the 19th hole for a real assessment of the event. It is estimated that there are more than 3,000 golf events each year. It feels like more.

From my personal and anecdotal research, here are the keys to a successful golf event:

- Don't put a non-golfer in charge of the golf event. Golf has many nuances that only a real golfer will understand and appreciate.
- Attend other golf outings in your area before you do your own. You can learn a lot from attending many other events—successful events, yes, but attend many unsuccessful events to really see how you can improve your strategy, goals, execution and results.
- Slow play is a bad thing. Avoid it by not loading up the course even if you will make more money; have something to entertain people before they go onto the par 3s (that is where most of the congestion is) such as messages, juice bar, a little combo, or food items.
- Sprinkle volunteers all over the course to find lost balls: the course pro will know where the key places are to position people.

- Hole-in-one opportunities are boring. I have attended probably 100 events and I have yet to see anyone win a car. I did, however, see someone shank a shot and put a dimple in a new Cadillac. Make it so more people win (and not a sleeve of balls) for landing on the green, landing in a sand trap, hitting into the water (these win boots or a ball finder).
- Create more fun flag events: longest drives and longest putts are old fashioned. Try adding some fun events that will bring new people to the winners' circle such as shortest off the tee, closest to the pin in four shots, most water shots, wildest t-shot on number 1 hole, craziest swing, and best golf bag.
- The real problem with golf events is that most people learn little or nothing about your organization during the event. Put fact boards on the tee-boxes that give information about the organization, or ask a question at the tee-box and have the answer at the hole. Make these as nice as your sponsor signs. Then they can be used year after year. Have several tee-box serving areas where people from your organization serve drinks or food and set up a display that only takes a few seconds to take in. You need to strike a balance of information and golf. Remember people do want to golf, so you don't want to get into the way of that activity. Make sure you meet and greet each golfer on the course. It's your event, so none of the top people should actually be golfing. Ride around in carts dropping off wet towels, water, sodas or candy.
- Make sure you have greeters at the parking lot as golfers arrive. The first few minutes of the event will set the tone for most people. If you appear organized and ready for golfers you will win over most events. Find a golf pro who really knows how to run these events. Shop around for the best venue.

What Is My Bid for this Auction?

Auctions, even if very successful are beginning to become a bit stale. Sure there are plenty of shining examples from wine auctions in Napa Valley to church auctions in Arlington Heights. Many garner nearly $100,000 in profit for the organizations. But for the most part auctions are the same from sea to shining sea. Committee volunteers find donated items from various retail outlets and businesses and hold a silent auction and live auction.

Auctions are marketing events. They tell a lot about your organization and may be the only time people interact with your organization. Auctions, like golf outings, need help to make them memorable events that raise money. At the least, these marketing events sell awareness and interest in your organization.

Reality Check

Before you cheer the next time you raise $25,000 to $50,000 on your auction do a reality check of your effort. Add up all your staff time devoted to this kind of event. Then divide the hours by the total raised. If the number is below $10 per hour, it is time to re-evaluate your effort. Had your staff people been meeting with individual contributors and asking for money, could they have raised the $25,000 without nickel-and-diming to death area businesses?

When you hold this kind of event you may find that your organization can't live without the money. It is better to do something big rather than make it part of the operating expense. All events wane with the years. If your operating expenses are tied to the event, who will you let go to make up for a bad year?

People also like to know they are doing some good. So make sure you have a clear goal and express it throughout the event. One 300-bed hospital selects a specific piece of equipment each year. This gives the fundraising event focus and helps target a goal for each event.

Everyone is a critic. But, how do you hold a successful auction and raise considerable funds as well as show how you are closing on the goal with each gift? Most benevolent people will enjoy seeing how they are impacting the gap on a thermometer of success. It will probably get people to up their bidding just to make milestones. For example, "this next item will put us over $50,000 for the night." That's better than saying, "we need to get $1,000 for this item."

Other areas include:

■ Get rid of the sports paraphernalia. We attended an auction and a Brett Farve helmet only went for $100 more than the price of a helmet from one of the sports-auction companies. Only include these kinds of items if you have many die-hard Green Bay fans. Otherwise they look interesting and exciting, but you won't get any money. Then you need to ship them back to the company. Too much work for too little return. I'm sure there are contrary stories, but why risk it? Take the $500 of investment and have a local artist make something spectacular that will generate interest, public relations and a lot of cash.

■ Establish some mini-sales opportunities throughout the night. Make sure you limit the sales and the time someone is forced to sell on each item. For example, have a couple work the crews for a treasure-chest grab bag. In the treasure chest are envelopes from $20 to $1,000 in coupons. Each person who pays $20 or more is entitled to select one envelope from the start. Most should include coupons that are worth more than the $20 fee. This can raise $400 to $1,400. The secret is in the people manning the store. If they are gregarious they will do well, if they are not, nothing will sell. Selling these kinds of packages can lead to a strong selling opportunity.

- Welcoming people at the door with greeters who encourage buying right from the start. Don't let people get off to a slow start. Get them into the swing early and often. But don't just sell items, sell the cause as well.

- Instill new life into your next auction. One mission-driven organization listed items on a screen and limited time for bids. People in the audience would write out bids and people would collect them and take them to the front. This process allowed people to socialize while the auction was going on.

- Work the crowd ahead of time. One way to guarantee income is to check with people days prior to the event. Finding a few people who will bid for items at a specific price will ensure a good event. If you think this is unethical, did you know that most telethons already know the tote-board totals before the night begins? You can't afford a disaster live in front of an audience.

- Alcohol seems to stimulate. Yet there is the obvious downside of excessive talking during the auction because of lubricated attendees. You may need to cut off the bar at some point and re-open after the auction is over.

- You must have bidders who are able to make a large contribution. You may need to have some people placed in the room to buy back an item if it is going too low.

- In a second room have some small bidding. At many of these events you will find a room where people have congregated to socialize and have a drink. Don't let them off the bidding hook. Have some smaller items ready and another group who might travel and get bids for items. Some people are hiding, so you may need to really persuade people to bid.

- Why have a dance afterwards? Too many times only the committee is remaining to dance. Maybe the band should be brought in early to get the people charged up. At the end, most people just want to pay and go home. Save the dance (and the money) for another event.

- Special items do sell, but you must find the right people. One-of-a-kind items also bring a high price tag. Send postcard announcements to likely bidders. Build the interest and pre-sell the price. At one auction I attend a priest builds a grandfather clock and donates it to the cause. It is a powerful item.

■ Hire a real auctioneer. There is something about the excitement and cadence of a real auctioneer. Real auctioneers need real spotters. These are people who move about the room working the crowd. If they are facing the auctioneer they have a problem. They should be looking at the room and working the crowd for more money.

Wine Tasting Events

O ne of the hottest fundraising events in many cities is wine or beer tasting. The experiential event usually has a very festive atmosphere, especially as the night progresses. The problem is getting the right people to the wine-tasting, not for the tasting, but for the buying of silent and live auction wine items.

I have not heard of this being done yet for mission-driven events, but I have seen these ideas done for others. They have tremendous possibilities for recruiting new people to the wine-tasting event.

When you line up your contributing wine distributor, work with the distributor's various retail outlets to allow you to place printed wine cards on selected bottles that will be featured at the wine-tasting event. You can buy these wine cards either with holes punched out so they go right over the neck of the bottle (the preferred way) or you can use string and attach a card. The card should tell the person that this bottle of wine will be available for tasting and the details about the wine-tasting event. This will get your advertising into the hands of people who buy wine. Perfect targeting. By selecting some of the higher-priced bottles, you can target people with higher incomes as well.

When looking for gifts for wine enthusiasts at the events a nice package is a printed wine wrap (to decorate the bottle and provide a place for a note) and a matching gift-card. The wine wrap is much preferred to the over-used wine bags. The package can carry your organization's logo subtly on the back. It is a way to give a bottle of wine to a friend and promote a worthy cause at the same time.

Wine does have its "wine snobs." I hope I'm not snobby, but I have tasted a lot of wines and own a lot of wines. You need to make sure you have a reserve section at your next wine-tasting. These wines will be more expensive, but you can charge extra for the chance to taste some premiere wines. In Napa Valley, many wineries have reserve tasting rooms. The reserve wine is made with specially-selected grapes and additional processing to bring out a richer flavor. There is an additional charge but it is always worth the additional price to those who care.

Look for a way to guarantee that you will have a high-value bottle for people to bid on. One organization called and e-mailed people from last year to see what kinds of wine and trips might be of interest before they started to look. This in some ways ensures an active bidder, because he or she is part of the selection process.

Wine and beer tastings can be a great way to raise funds, but don't try to have too long a program, especially at the end of the evening. You will need to contend with loud-talking and disinterested party-goers.

One area you may want to address is a driving service to make sure all you contributors get home safely and without an incident. (I'm assuming you have adequate insurance, but be careful with these events). You can advertise it in advance and charge extra or have it available after the event. I prefer the advance knowledge because you can have enough limos lined up and prepaid service. In fact, you may just want to offer pick up and delivery service for an additional fee. It could really help boost your income with very little work.

Fundraising

"Donors don't give to institutions. They invest in ideas and people in whom they believe."
G.T. Smith

Fundraising and Marketing

This is not a book on fundraising. However, at mission-driven organizations fundraising and marketing go hand-in-hand. For many groups, fundraising is the only marketing they do in a given year. Still, it is important to remember that fundraising communications are marketing. The nice part is that you have a clear return on investment expectation with fundraising that cannot be achieved with branding and other advertising for your organization. That is, unless you can afford to conduct market studies each year.

Nearly every mission-driven organization can raise funds, and it is one of the key benefits of being a 501c-3 organization. At the heart of any organization is the annual campaign. Unfortunately, these are carried out at specific times during the year, most in the fourth quarter. I realize that United Way does have a blackout period if you are receiving funds from the United Way. But, for the sake of discussion, I'm going to assume there is no United Way blackout period. Also, we will not explore capital campaigns as part of this chapter. Capital campaigns are a highly specialized effort that requires a book of its own.

First and Foremost You Need a Theme

Your fundraising effort needs a theme every year. I'm not talking about just a catchy slogan or cute metaphor. This theme needs to touch people in real and meaningful ways. It needs to involve potential and current contributors at an emotional level.

The theme really needs to answer the question, "Why have annual campaigns at all?" Themes do help tie together campaigns. But the real key to a theme's success is consistency. The theme should permeate all materials. For example, if your theme is "Setting the Gold Standard" and you can only afford to print in black and white, change the theme. There will be a disconnect with contributors and the overall message will suffer.

It is estimated that we are bombarded with some 3,000 messages per day. If your theme does not resonate with your publics, is not consistent, or does not have enough frequency, then it is doomed to fail. Worse yet, it will be ignored.

The theme should not be decided lightly. A great theme should last for years until it stops working. So, design your theme to be powerful enough to last a few years. If it doesn't work, change it. If it does work, don't change it until it stops working. The calendar shouldn't force marketing decisions.

Finally, the theme must be true and real. Many colleges use the tag line "A Tradition of Excellence." Yet if you walk on to these campuses today you can find places where the tradition has come to a screeching halt or the excellent tradition never started. The theme must be real and true to connect with people.

Challenge the notion that people are not interested in giving to operations.

It's true that many times large donors and foundations would rather give to something tangible such as a building rather than to operations. This may have to do with ensuring how the money is used rather than the notion that people don't like to give to operations.

One foundation intimated that when they give to operations the organizations come back every year. With a building, organizations usually space out their visits. The Red Cross received millions after 9/11. All of the money was for operations. Millions poured into Florida after the hurricanes. United Way is still one of the largest annual fund campaigns in communities and it is all targeted for operations. Is it hard to raise money for operations? Sure, but this has more to do with the case and the way of asking than the reason for giving.

Imagine if the effort of a new building capital campaign was put into an annual fund drive. There would be a case statement with a compelling strategy, events throughout the year, staff priorities, endorsements, phone banks, donor visits, public relations efforts, and video, CD-ROMs, recognition, and follow-up. What would be the results? Strong "operational" stories or, better yet, strong reasons to give to annual funds are what are missing from most annual funds. Imagine if each annual appeal effort was handled as a mini-capital campaign rather than "an annual appeal mailing."

Are You Sending the Same Message to Younger and Older Donors?

Annual giving is at the base of the fundraising pyramid. This is where you will identify the future major supporters of the organization. Annual giving requires a macro view of the world: you need to reach as large a population as you can and then work these givers to higher levels of giving each year.

So, are you sending the same mailing to a 30-year-old as you're sending to someone who voted for Richard Nixon, is on their third mortgage, has two kids and is in their second marriage? You must segment your annual fund mailings by age groups. If you don't, it would be the equivalent of Hot Topic and JC Penny collaborating on a catalogue. No one would win and the result would not attract either audience. The message must be audience-centered in order to connect.

For these young donors (and non-donors) the emphasis should be on giving—at any level—and not on dollars. Establishing a 'giving habit' is more important than the amount.

- Set the contribution-card giving options low: $5, $10, $15, $25 and $100.
- Have the letter come from a peer in the age category (not a famous person, but an average person facing the same problems).
- Make the envelope look official, something along the lines of a notice from a student loan.
- Explain how even a small gift can make a big difference for those in need.
- Establish a recognition area on the Web site that lists all new contributors. Give these people a little taste of the joy of giving, and the resulting recognition. Make sure this is instantaneous on the Web with a follow-up e-mail to the contributor that the gift has been posted for all to see.
- Encourage consecutive years of giving as a goal. Create special recognition levels based on years of giving and not dollars. Also, allow people to buy back past missed years.
- Include an incentive in all mailings. This group is not different than any other group, they love something free. This group is more likely to display a gift from you because the younger age group has not accumulated as much to display in an office setting. So keep the 'newbie' office place in mind when formulating ideas for incentives.

Here's a novel idea. Stop calling the annual fund the annual fund. The notion that people like to give one time a year is the same as thinking that car buyers buy the total price of a car. Most people buy monthly payments—from homes to furniture to cars. Why else would 0% financing be so attractive?

Why then does giving need to be on an annual basis? Giving should be monthly. There is an old trick that insurance salespeople use; it's called *reducing to the absurd*. Instead of saying that a policy costs $100 a year (annual gift) it costs just pennies a day. Can't you just hear the salesperson saying "isn't your family's security worth just pennies a day?"

Online banking is making giving monthly a snap. A few minutes to type in your address and then the person can set up payment every month. It's just like payroll deduction but without all the paperwork.

Encouraging monthly giving means that you must change how you position your letters and contribution card. Instead of $1,000 per annual gift, you would list $84 per month. Monthly giving also has another benefit—12 thank you notes to a contributor. That is great frequency, but don't send the same letter each month.

Online Banking

Online banking is growing rapidly. There is an area on most online banking that is called the "payee area." There are lists of payees that already have information listed with the institution. This makes giving just a click away. Otherwise the person must type in all the information and set up your organization as a payee. The benefits to online banking are:

1) *It is convenient for the contributor;*
2) *It can encourage large gifts by spreading them monthly instead of one-time gifts;*
3) *There is no need for a postage stamp.*

There may be a way to work with banks (for a price of course) to include them on the contribution card and encourage online banking and contributing at the same time.

"Land's End" Approach

Today, we are faced with a hyper-marketed world. Nowhere is this more prevalent than in direct mailing. The only way you can compete and break through is to turn up the volume.

In advertising we talk about reach and frequency. A commercial first must be seen by a potential audience, and that is called the *reach* or how many people total will see your ad. Then we talk about *frequency*. For most ads we are encouraging a frequency of "5" or more. In other words, the potential prospect must see an ad five or more times before it will sink in and stand out from the marketing clutter.

How this relates to direct mail is simple. Gone are the days of one giant catalogue sent out once a year. Now direct marketers send out multiple catalogues throughout the year. Sometimes, it is the same catalogue, just a different cover. This is the "Land's End" effect.

This approach realizes how people live. They are busy. They are not paying attention. So how do you utilize the "Land's End" approach to fundraising? It is another perception shift: It means that the annual fund letter really is not "a" letter at all. It is now a "series of touches" with the potential donor base. This also allows you to better test different appeals approaches during the year, from carrier envelopes to postcards, from CD-ROM to e-mail, from color to black and white.

Not ready to begin this aggressive approach? How else do you think you are going to get the non-giving public to give to you? One letter to your targeted non-giving donor market is not enough. Once a person moves from non-giving to giving then you can move to a different cultivation approach. It's getting that first gift that is so difficult. Getting that first order for Land's End I'm sure has the same level of difficulty.

Different Strokes for Different Folks

Personalization is a buzz-word in the new age of digital marketing, data bases and digital printing. Putting names throughout a letter or in design elements can help personalize a direct mail piece in new ways never before imagined. You will find this approach requires 20 to 30 percent more in printing costs. The simple, non-tech way of personalization is to have different appeals for different groups. I have already suggested age differences, but segmenting your potential giving and current giving population needs more attention. The days of blanket-appeal letters should be dead. Sit down with your list and break it into different categories of people. Pick any information that you are gathering. Here is a very simple listing.

Non Givers (Younger)
Non Givers (Older)
Givers New the last few years
Givers ($1 to $250)
Givers ($250 to $1,000)
Givers ($1,000 and up)
Board members

Past board members
Purchased list of homes with household incomes of $100,000 or more

Now write letters, design contribution cards and include information that speaks directly to these targeted groups. Any business will tell you that it is easier and less costly to grow current clients than it is to find new ones. The only problem with that is without new clients you will slowly go out of business. Segmentation will allow you to better focus your message but keep the theme consistent. At the least the salutation and first line should be personalized.

For example, "Don, as a board member you know . . ."

Build Competition between Groups

Everyone loves a little friendly competition. Build goals based on a group's past giving. Take board members and challenge them to give 10 percent more than last year. One way to help keep the challenge going is to build giving thermometers on your Web site. Sending the board members to check the Web site to see how their gifts stack up with last year or other years will help keep the competition lively and foster second gifts from individuals to help win. So, in our example of the theme "Setting the Gold Standard," you may have two giving years that were record-setting: a bronze and silver level of giving, and your gold level is this year's goal. Follow-up postcards can work to help capture a one-day snapshot of the thermometer and drive people to the Web to check out the new level. This effort would be especially effective if you have online giving facilitated by instant gratification. A donor makes a gift and can see the thermometer rise. Now that is interaction.

Build Urgency into Your Gift Asks

By setting up some competition you can build urgency into your asks without using IRS advantage as the only reason. Ask some of your larger givers to make challenge gifts for various areas. For example, you might have a $10,000 Valentine's Children Challenge to help raise money and send a special Valentine with a Dairy Queen coupon to all unfortunate children in the area. Then, send out targeted postcards (or use writing on the outside of the envelope) to put urgency into the challenge gifts appeal. This will help add time-pressure into some of your giving, no matter how small the challenge. Examples of urgency-messages might be: *"Only two more weeks before we lose the challenge gift."* Or, *"Only a few weeks left on doubling your contribution."* Or, *"We want to send a Valentine treat to all poor kids in the area, your gift will make it happen but there's only two weeks to Valentine's Day."*

Too many times in fundraising we rely on the calendar and the threat of losing a tax deduction to force giving. Allow your challenge gifts to apply pressure to non-givers throughout the year. Experiment with postcards to compel use of your online pledge forms. The postcards are inexpensive to mail and can give a time-sensitive feel to the challenge gift.

All great negotiators use *time pressure*. Now it's time to use a little time pressure to build your annual fund throughout the year.

Fundraising Thank-you Notes

You cannot thank someone too many times for a gift. But, because of technology and the legal requirements of charity laws, those thank-you letters are beginning to look like IRS-approved notices rather than true, heartfelt thank-you notes. Build into your giving plan having volunteers (with good penmanship) write hand-written thank-you notes. Personalization is the key. If you work for an organization with children, have the kids make some thank-you notes or cards. Even if all they write is "Mr. Mathis, thank you for helping me, Tommy," I know that it would touch many people right in the heart. Space out your thank-you notes so that you have frequency and some unexpected surprises for people as well. Two months after someone makes a gift would be an excellent time to write a second thank-you note. Who knows, it may prompt a second gift and a new round of thank-you efforts.

What about a thank-you phone-a-thon? However, don't raise money, raise the awareness that your organization is truly appreciative of contributions. What a shock it would be for people to receive a thank-you call that doesn't ask for something in return.

One way to do this is to use a calling service that leaves messages on voicemail machines. The call price is approximately 15 to 25 cents per call. The voice can be anyone you wish: a board member, a child, a grateful patient. The calls all go out at once in the space of an hour. Politicians use this to great effect during the election. Keep it simple and very conversational so that it doesn't sound like a sales pitch. The key is that it should not irritate people the same way a begging call does. It can have some star power, depending on who you have record the message, and it can be saved and played for the other members of the household.

And if I haven't said it enough, thank you for reading this book.

Annual Report Online

Printed annual reports of contributors serve as an important recognition vehicle for donors. Do not cancel these just because you think the Web will be the next hit. Don't underestimate the power of a good annual report and how it is used throughout the year when visiting with potential donors and recognizing your best contributors.

This is the Internet age, so there may be some other new recognition solutions that are more in line with the times. At least you should begin to experiment with new media. Establish an online report that is not annual. In other words, on your Web site make a donor recognition area that can immediately recognize people as they make a contribution. You can then direct people to the Web site in your thank-you note. The site could include a complete listing of contributors on a virtual recognition wall. You could also make the database searchable allowing people to see who contributed from different categories or areas or cities. You could feature contributors throughout the year with a photo area, post pictures of the recipients of contributed dollars, such as kids holding signs that say thank-you and the name of the donor, or start a bulletin-board area to answer questions.

One way to utilize this highly pliable technology would be to build a listing throughout the year of projects or items that you need contributions to provide. If you're a YMCA you might have on the list: Four Basketballs $200, Whistles for Volunteer Coaches $25.00 and Scholarship for Camps $275.00. Then when a contributor has selected the item, it lights up and the contributor's name is added to the area. The best part is that this list would be fluid throughout the year representing your true needs. You can send out reminder postcards when you get close to a particular date (with camp scholarships the date might be March 30) to add urgency. You might post, "We need three more camp scholarships to make our goal. Please visit the YMCA Wish List and help make a dream come true for a child." This area needs a real special feel compared to your regular Web site, but this kind of medium can be much more fluid than the printed kind. More importantly, it can provide *instant gratification* for contributors.

Just imagine the process of someone making a contribution and in your thank-you back you tell the person that their gift has been posted on the Wall of Contributors at *www.yourOrganization.Org/greatpeople*. Then you also post on the Web site near their name a photograph of a kid holding a sign that says "Thank you Mr. Mathis." Wow, you've got me hooked for a gift every year.

Beware of the Non-Salesperson Fundraising

Fundraising is sales. For the enlightened, this is a truth that helps propel organizations to new heights. Bad salespeople make bad fundraisers. I'm not talking about a car salesperson. I'm talking about salespeople who are required to go out and prospect for new clients. Beware of the fundraiser who spends too much time on the materials and tools of fundraising and not on contacts. You'll spot them immediately, they are constantly getting ready to make calls, but don't make them. If a person could see two people a day that is more than 500 people per year. Because of those meetings if their collective giving could increase 50 percent, then the average gift of $500 would equal a return on investment of $125,000. That is a good payback on the time invested. Can you meet with 500 people? If you did, what would happen to your organization? The PR value would be incredible: the giving would be dramatic as well. Don't let your next fundraising person wait for a capital campaign before going to visit with constituents.

Many salespeople are required to fill out call reports. It is simply a listing of who the person called that week and what the next action will be. You could even use a sales program such as Goldmine to keep track of the calls and subsequent action. Sure, there are plenty of giving software packages, but contact software is contact software. You can use an Excel spread-sheet and accomplish the same results. The key is that the calls are made every day.

When I started the St. Francis Healthcare Foundation my goal was to raise my salary and pay all the expenses of the new foundation. I remember some advice I was given by a successful fundraiser. He said to pick a range of giving and then go and meet the people. His suggestion was to not ask for money, but simply share with the contributors about what is going on at the hospital, making sure to thank the contributors for their past gifts. I looked at my meager list and I picked anyone who had given $100 to the hospital for any reason and started making calls. Most didn't want to see me, but many sent a gift in shortly after my call. Those who did meet with me increased their giving dramatically. One woman I visited lived in a home I would describe as "modern decrepit." The neighborhood made me afraid to leave my car. I sat in my car debating if I was going to go up to the door. She had agreed to meet with me on the phone, but she still made me stand outside the door for about five minutes. Once she decided I was okay and not "selling something" she invited me in. We talked about the failing neighborhood, her beautiful paintings and the state of healthcare. She served me coffee and cookies. I talked to her a bit about what the foundation's goals were. After two hours, I thanked her again for being so generous. Two weeks later, a $1,000 check arrived at the foundation. She became one of the top contributors to our tiny foundation with that one gift.

That little story should be a reminder to us all that, first, you should never pre-qualify anyone until you've met with them; and second, people give to (and buy) from people they like and trust. You can't build trust on the Internet, in letters or on the phone. You need to meet face-to-face.

People who give year after year are excellent prospects for a visit. If you don't know why they give so regularly, then it is definitely time for a visit. Don't make the mistake of making a huge presentation. Just visit, listen for giving cues, and be sure to thank the person.

Guerrilla Marketing

"Smart marketers use every technique available to gain a foothold in the consumer's mind. With guerrilla marketing, the focus changes from the volume of advertising to the impact of the message."
Jay Levinson
The Guerrilla Marketing Handbook

Guerrilla Marketing Efforts

A lot has been written about "guerrilla" marketing techniques. It does sound sexy to act like a Contra rebel, hiding in the bush and pouncing on your marketing prey. The problem is really all that changes is the focus: you exchange reach for impact. In other words you reach fewer people, but, when you do reach them, you have a greater chance for results.

Most guerrilla techniques require two things: an idea and time. Because you're "hitting" people where they live or work and in small numbers, the results can be hard to track on a large scale. So it takes more time for these efforts to show substantial results.

Guerrilla marketers are obsessed with selling benefits. Benefits are the key to any marketing effort, but they are super-duper important in the guerrilla world. Major companies use guerrilla techniques with great results. New liquors trying to break into the market will hire models to go to the hottest nightclubs. When men approach the models they order the targeted brand. Men will order more of the brand for other women, and women will order the brand to emulate the models. Or new video-game companies will send new game-boxes to one person on a college dorm floor for free with the one stipulation that he or she will invite people to his or her room to play.

Guerrilla tactics are not cheap. The cost per person is usually much higher than traditional marketing efforts. But the results can be very dramatic. Guerrilla techniques have a high risk-reward quotient.

Proof-of-Performance Cards

"In the future, everyone will be world famous for fifteen minutes."
Andy Warhol

W hen a mountain climber reaches the peak what are the first things he or she will do? The mountaineer plants a flag and takes a picture, usually with the mountain climber in the photo. It is a proof of performance. "I told you I was going to climb a mountain and here is a photograph of me and my buddies at the top to prove it," the photo attests.

The same concept works for businesses and service organizations. When you finish a major project, or ascend a goal, let people know about it. It proves out your performance for all to see. Some organizations do send out cards and announcements about very large projects such as capital campaigns and building projects. But this is not enough to give people a strong feeling that your organization is moving in a forward direction. The key is not in one card; the true power is in the many cards received during a given year. In other words, it is frequency. Frequency combined with consistency can build grand canyons or move public opinion.

Pick your top six accomplishments over the past year. Develop 12, 6 X 9-inch postcards and print them all at the same time. This is called gang-printing and can dramatically cut the cost of printing. Then, every month, send a card to each key stakeholder.

Let's say you successfully finished an accreditation process. Send out a card announcing your accreditation, why it is important and how well you did on the project. There may be some verbiage from the accreditation organization that you will want to quote in the postcard. The copy can be short. You just want the person to register that you promised to do something, you did it, and you excelled: it is your proof of performance. You need to be careful not to brag, but to offer as straightforward a report as possible. Remember to make the key points beneficial to the stakeholder. For example, "We helped kids stay in school so fewer will be going to prison, cutting costs to tax-payers and making our state safer."

Your Sign Should Say More

"So I got me a pen and a paper, and I made up my own little sign."
Signs
Five Man Electrical Band

Developing the proper signage is a lost art. Most sign companies have a 20-year-old with little experience designing signs, and it shows. Unfortunately it shows on more mission-driven and local business signs because these are designed "in house." The national signs are designed and tested before they go up.

It just seems like most mission-driven signs are designed so that they don't follow any of the rules of advertising. Your sign probably gets the most reach of any marketing materials you produce. That is, of course, unless you use mass media.

A president of an organization that works with disabled people once told me that "people don't know who we are or what we do." He was so upset because they had been on fundraising calls in his home city and two of the people contacted had never heard of his organization. I didn't want to tell him that I couldn't find his offices and had to be "talked-in" by the receptionist. His sign was so small that it was impossible to see driving at 30 mph.

It's time to rethink your sign. A sign is so important because it gives your organization "place." This is that feeling one gets about a business or organization when one knows where their building is. It makes your organization more real, provides credibility and gives you a true local connection to the community. This only works when the community knows where you are. Your signs work for you 24-hours-a-day, seven days a week; every holiday, in rain and snow.

Your sign can work even harder than other media because this is the likely place a television crew will do a live shot or the newspaper will probably file your sign shot for future stories about your organization. Almost everyone puts their building photo with the sign prominently displayed on their Web site.

The problem with signs is that they are expensive and need maintenance. This is why most people skimp on their signs. Your sign is your "face" to a lot of people and it says a lot about what kind of organization you are. Does your sign say you are successful? People who give big money like to give to successful organizations. Does your sign say what you do? How will anyone learn about you if your sign doesn't tell them?

You may be thinking that your building is on an infrequently-traveled road with little visibility. One hospital administrator got by that by renting space on a building near an Interstate exit ramp. It was a directional sign to his hospital. It was large and loud. And if competing in healthcare were a chess game, he had just declared checkmate. Find space to put your sign; put it up on a pole so people can see it from all directions and all surrounding streets. There are city codes to follow of course. But if the codes get in the way of your communicating, hire an attorney and push for a variance.

If you have a building that is adjacent to two streets make sure you get two signs. Think communications. Think like a car dealer. This is no time to be "understatedly elegant," because you must bust through the clutter.

Consider making signs with two sides instead of running signs perpendicular to the street. You want to use a billboard mentality when placing your signs. Signs in a "V" shape work the best so that people can easily see them from either direction as they travel.

How much can you say on a sign? Remember, people will be driving by your sign so you need to use the "rule for billboards." Use only seven words. These seven include your name and branding line. Make sure your branding-line says something about your organization that is easily understood. If your sign is near a traffic-light where people must wait for a minute or two, you can put more on your sign. If there is no stop light, then you must make sure you are under the seven-word limit.

When you are making key decisions about your sign, make sure you put enough in the budget to light your sign. Otherwise, you lose the best time for a sign which is at night. Signs show up at night better because the background has dropped out of the picture. There is higher contrast against a black sky. Night also tends to be the most highly-traveled time when, during the winter months, people go to and from work and school events, and they are on standard time. Make sure that your Web site has a prominent place on your sign. This is not part of the seven words, but you must have an easy-to-read and easy to remember URL to make it work. Remember to capitalize real words in your URL. For example www.AmericanRedCross.org is a lot easier to read than www.americanredcross.org. The capital letters will not have any impact on the address.

Name Your Processes

In many markets there is more than one mission-driven organization providing the same or similar services. Big Brothers/Big Sisters, the YMCA, and a host of child-welfare agencies are all providing services to "troubled" children. Technically, these are all very different service lines with clearly defined missions, but to contributors and the general public they are all part of the same "services-to-kids pot."

There may be room in the market for several organizations, but there is only room for one "perceived" leader in the market since marketing is a perception game. You want to be the leader because that is where the top board members, foundations and contributors want to invest resources. We all like to give to a winner.

One way to distinguish yourself from the competition is to name the processes in your organization. One of the complaints many people have about service organizations is that it seems as if the problems, from hunger to broken homes, are never improving. Sure, you must show a need before people will give, but they also want to know that something is working. We've already discussed how important names are to an organization: however the benefit to naming your process is to give current and future supporters a sense that what you do is proven and delivered in a consistent manner. The name says that a specific process has been researched, tested and works.

We want your systems to be "proprietary processes." In other words, *only* Org X owns and provides this process. One sure way to do this is to register the name of your plan with the state and secure a service-mark or trademark. Service-marks are state registrations and usually cost between $25 and $50. You do not need an attorney to register your name with your state, and you can then put "SM" in superscript next to your name. This will visually set off your plan from others and give it instant credibility. I like to call this the *Mathis Process of Marketing Management*^sm system of overall enhancement of your marketing. This is only an example for demonstration purposes, but notice how, suddenly, the name with the service-mark designation gave this idea form and a more formal feeling.

This may sound contrary to the chapter on naming your organization, but you don't need to worry too much about the name of your process. Most people will not remember the name, but they will remember that you possess propriety rights to a process that is achieving results.

So at a speech to the Rotary Club, you can describe your working with kids to improve self-esteem and to teaching kids to respect themselves, or you can begin with the Org X Confidence-Builder Power Plan^sm.

A "plan" is a method of accomplishing an objective or goal. Plan also implies a means to a positive, specific end. It also implies that if your plan isn't followed, clients may not succeed. PLAN needs an action-word to give it punch and more importantly, memorability. The word POWER is defined by Webster's Dictionary as "the ability to act or produce an effect." This is the number one definition for the word "power," and that is exactly what the OrgX program provides.

"Power" and "Plan" together provide a nice alliteration as well. In advertising, that makes a large difference as to whether something is remembered or not. This may seem a lot like the Wizard of Oz, but it a proven method to add credibility to your processes. I'm not asking you to lie about your process for helping people. If you don't have any proven processes, then don't make them up. I'm only suggesting that you name the processes to give them some marketing punch.

Become Your Own Advertiser with a Billboard on Your Land

If you're having trouble finding a budget for advertising, it may be as close as your land. If you own land or a building on a busy thoroughfare, investigate if you can erect your own billboard. It will give you free space to put up as many messages as you think are necessary. The only cost would be for installation of the new boards and flex-vinyl.

There are city code issues, but your local billboard company may help you through the process, especially if they can sell the back side of the board. This could be a revenue generator for your organization as well. On a two-sided billboard, you take one side for your messages, and work out a revenue-sharing plan for the other side with the billboard company. Don't try to sell the space yourself: the billboard company has the installers, the contacts and the insurance to make this work. If you try to sell the space it could sit open for many months.

Even if you can't put up a billboard, if enough eyeballs pass by your building you may be able to do a large building wrap or giant banner. The building wraps are mostly used in large cities, but in smaller cities and towns they could generate not only a lot of talk throughout the community, but some PR as well if you can get the press to cover your new approach to getting the word out about your good works.

AD-Mails/Flash Animations

There is a new technique that is highly effective for communicating with e-mails. There is not a good name for these so I've dubbed them "AD-mails." The concept consists of attaching a flash-animation message or mini-video to your e-mail or linking the e-mail to your Web site where you house many animations. These animations are really mini-videos or commercials about various parts of your organization.

This means two things: 1) you are collecting e-mail addresses of your key stakeholders and 2) you have something to say. The key to this communications is that e-mail is growing exponentially as a key communication vehicle for business. But, with the daunting mass of e-mail that people receive, it is difficult to break through the electronic clutter.

One way to do this is flash-animations and mini-video electronic messages to tell, and more importantly, show people what you do. These AD-mails are an excellent way to give your business a high-tech, progressive look with a high-touch visual component to the message.

There will be a cost for each AD-mail. But the nice part is that you can add to your list each quarter and spread out the costs while building your message. Imagine coming back from a donor-call where the person said they were interested in children and preschool education. You could then send an e-mail thank-you with the link to an AD-mail that speaks specifically about preschool education at your organization. At the end of the AD-mail is a place for the person to click on to make a contribution expressly to that part of your organization. Now that is follow-through. But it doesn't stop there: if the person wants to forward your AD-mail to friends, then it becomes viral marketing.

Colleges that use this technique also include flash-animations for birthdays and other holidays. These can be sent by anyone, so it enhances the viral possibilities as well. Short testimonials can also be incorporated into the animations further supporting the sales effort.

Some companies, with extensive databases also send flash-animations on significant events: customer birthdays, company anniversaries, end-of-year congratulations, awards and other recognition. The goal is to set up a personalized, yet automated effort to let people know your company is thinking about them even though there is not a current sale.

These animations can either be embedded in the e-mail or linked to your Web site. The salesperson would have access to all and select the product they would like to feature in any correspondence.

Audio Moniker

When I worked at an NBC affiliate, many times a day I would hear three familiar musical notes—these were G-E-C. The notes stood for General Electric Company, but the notes of the NBC chimes, as they were called, were as synonymous with the company as the peacock logo. Without looking up at the television set you knew you had NBC on your television.

Today, audio-branding is as important as the logo, color and logotype. Even a computer chip manufacturer used the NBC technique to brand that Intel was inside. Do we really need to know that Intel's inside? Isn't it a little like knowing the brand of carburetor in a car? Yes and yes. It is important for Intel; every time the notes sound for Intel at the end of computer ads it brands the chips as important, but it also sends a strong message to investors that this is a good stock to buy.

ESPN and Monday Night Football have distinctive sounds that many people have downloaded to their cell phones to use as rings. All these uses help further brand ESPN and Monday Night Football.

The AFLAC duck could also be considered an audio-brand moniker, because the duck saying AFLAC is distinctive and fun to say.

Even Harley Motorcycles is trying to patent its distinctive rumbling sound. Harley believes that the sound of the Harley is so valuable that it is worth protecting it from copycats and that it is distinctive enough to be a reason people buy the bikes.

So, use an audio moniker with your advertising: television, radio, on-hold messages, opening of your business meetings, and a sound that goes off when your front door is opened. It should be used at employee and stakeholder events. The key is to make sure that the "moniker" is used over and over again. Frequency builds the idea that the sound is your sound: just like a logo must be seen again and again in order to be connected with the business.

The secret to an audio "moniker" is its simplicity. Most are only three to five notes long. The more notes, the less distinctive it will be, though you don't need to always use notes to set up an audio "moniker." Sounds can also be effective: a child's laugh, song bird singing, wind chimes, door bells. The list is endless. What is important is that the sound is distinctive, and relates to your organization or its mission.

Grade Your System for PR Recognition

The press loves grading systems. Major examples are the terrorism color system or national educational rating system. The "grades" organizations receive are very easy to report and simple for anyone to understand. When it is reported that your educational system received a C, you know exactly what that means, or at least you know there is considerable room for improvement.

The hardest part in establishing a grading system is to make its criteria valid. So, you will need to develop a comprehensive grading scale that can be easily digested and neutral. Once you've completed the criteria, it is time to rate and rank the effort you want to test. For example, if we were trying to rate child welfare conditions in your state, we would want strong, no nonsense criteria for the rankings. Once you've completed the grading of the service or provider, it is then time to release the information. It may be a good idea to share this ranking with the parties you are about to rate. If, for example, it is for the Department of Human Service and you get all your money through referrals from them, you may want to make sure the DHS is ready for a response.

The press may not cover it at the time you conduct this survey, however, in future years they will be more likely to pick it up once they know this is not a one-shot effort. Make the ranking a semi-annual release with updated information—the timing of which should coincide with the legislative session.

A Thermometer of the Underserved

The problem with many mission-driven causes is that the cause is very hard to visualize. It is not a convenient product with a well-defined set of parameters. Most are the softer side of marketing because most deliver services.

Every year, towns across the country use United Way thermometers of giving. Many times, a community will prominently display a large thermometer and update the progress of the campaign. Newspapers regularly run the thermometer graphic with or without stories. It is a tangible, visual way to tell the story of United Way giving each year—and each year it looks like a new story.

Your story is just as important. Create a thermometer of the underserved in your community: it could be the number of children not receiving court-ordered care; the number of heart attacks in your area; the number of children without a family; or the number of people waiting on the organ donation list. It's time to put our problems into a number that will change from week to week or month to month. The more change the better. People will check back more regularly if the changes happen on a weekly basis.

The question is, "where to put this thermometer?" My first choice would be on a rotary billboard in the best location in town. There is no use in going to all this trouble and not have people see it. However, if your building is in a prominent location with good visibility then you can mount it there. You may also find a friendly business who will rent space or give you space for your "thermometer of the underserved."

If you ever go to Birmingham, Alabama, you will see a statue high up on a hill. It is called the Vulcan. When the Vulcan's torch is green, there has not been a traffic accident in Birmingham for 24 hours. If it is red, then there has been a death. It is an excellent reminder to be careful on the roads as you drive through the town. Your thermometer should have the same effect on people who drive by to help build your buzz marketing. You will want people telling other people to go by your billboard to see the number.

Once the thermometer is up and operational, it's time for the public relations mechanism to kick in. Working with the press you can get coverage for the day you put up the thermometer and again when the thermometer reaches milestones—good and bad milestones.

Ideally, you can show this thermometer on your Web site either as a graphic that is updated, or by posting a Web-cam pointed at your billboard to show live photos of the thermometer. Every time you update the billboard e-mails could be sent to friends of your organization, legislators and local politicians linking them to the live Web cam.

Create an Award to Remember

People will say that awards are meaningless and that they just don't matter—until they win one. Then everyone crows a bit. One way to create buzz in your service category is to hold an annual award. If you want to create buzz in healthcare offices about your organization create a nursing award; if you want teachers talking, create a teacher award; if you want business people talking, create a young business person award.

Many of these categories receive little in the way of recognition. The awards provide a wonderful press publicity opportunity, but more importantly they create a positive environment for buzz-marketing to take hold with a key audience.

For you to capture the imagination of a cynical public, a skeptical press and "seen-all-the-motivational-techniques" target audience, you will need a prize that will grab attention.

I would suggest a substantial prize—cash is the best. A $1,000 to $2,000 cash prize will provide the stimulus to let people know that you are serious about recognizing your target audience. Have a glamorous trophy made that includes your name and logo in a prominent place: Large trophies make great photographs in newspapers, in the recipient's office newsletter and in your new postcard newsletter. The trophies will probably be displayed in the recipient's business further giving you exposure to key markets.

It is recommended that you create an awards committee made up of peers from the target audience you are focusing on. This will give you instant credibility with people in related fields. Provide this committee with the responsibility to come up with the award criteria, judging requirements and judges.

This is a perfect Monday-release story for those slow news days. You will be able to set your own criteria for the award and the call for nominations should be a media-worthy event as well. There will be some expense for the trophy, cash prize, advertising for nominations and nomination forms.

If you have a regular event you can make the presentation then, or you can hold a special lunch banquet. However, I would rather see you spend more on the prize and trophy than on the lunch. One way to provide a good award venue without the expense is to partner with another group's event, announcing and recognizing the winner there. Rotary, Exchange Clubs, Kiwanis and other groups need many programs. Your award could be an exciting presentation and put you in front of many community-minded business people.

Try to tie your awards into national specially-designated days, weeks or months for the category. For nurses, the National Nurse Week is in May.

Paint Automobiles

W hen I worked for a television station, and part of a seven-station broadcast group, the "marking" of vehicles had been richly debated for years. Some news directors didn't want the cars marked so the reporters could sneak up on stories. The promotion people wanted to mark them so that all in the town would know that the station was there doing a story. Even if the people didn't watch they would know that station was in their town.

Then one day as I drove home from work I followed a Hy-Vee Grocery Store flower delivery van on the Interstate and I was struck by the simple power of the medium.

How did I know it was a Hy-Vee flower van? In fact, how did I know Hy-Vee delivered flowers at all? The larger-than-life photo of roses that adorned every side of the van gave me all the information I needed. And, even though I passed the van at a high rate of speed, I got the message loud and clear in just a few seconds. I knew Hy-Vee delivered flowers every day and their phone number screamed it out loud.

Many would look at those flowers and think they are too big, too loud, too much. Some would even say that their organizations are above *loud and literal* signage on their vehicles. However, in today's hyper-marketing world, there is no time to be understatedly elegant. This is not the information age, it is the *visual* age. You have a short period of time to make an impression visually: you cannot squander any and all opportunities—especially unexpected opportunities for little costs.

Once you've decided your branding color, then paint your fleet that color or buy all vehicles in that color. This will help your vehicles stand out in a crowd, parking-lot or highway. Yes it will cost more. Yes, it will not be as easy as purchasing vehicles in the past. And no, you don't need "variety" in your vehicles. What you need is someone with the strong-armed marketing discipline to make your marketing dollars go farther. Don't relegate the purchase of vehicles to someone who doesn't understand the power of consistent marketing.

Let's say you have a few vans in your fleet. Now, think of these vans as billboards. They are approximately the same size as most boards and they reach people on the roadways. So, when you're buying your van you're really buying a billboard for everyday of the year—without a monthly media expense. In fact, there are companies that make a good living placing billboards on the semi-trailers that crisscross the country. Now is the time for you to take advantage of this free-media space. When your van becomes a billboard, the name of your organization must be large, loud, proud and consumed in two to three seconds of attention. Include your branding-line and your Web site. Remember to put all the information on both sides and the back of the vehicles as well. There are many ways to do this. You can have this information painted on or you can use the new photo transfer-wraps to put your message on your vehicle.

At John Deere would you expect any color van other than green? Should the Duke Blue Devils drive up in a red bus? Then, why would it not make sense for your organization to bring marketing to the roadways of your community?

When American Airlines took over TWA they painted every plane in American colors. The reason was so that American visually dominated an area of the airport. When you look around St. Louis, you don't think there is another airline besides AA.

Color is powerful. Use your fleet to market your color, your name and your brand. Marking your vehicles is just one way to get a firm hand on the marketing wheel of your organization and go for a ride on the brand-consistent road.

Power of Thank-you Notes

An integral part of our marketing company is a fundraising division. Surprisingly, to those who don't understand communications, fundraising and marketing go hand-in-glove. In fundraising, we suggest that you thank your contributors seven times—at a minimum. In fact, I don't think you can ever over-thank someone.

The only thing better than a thank-you letter, is a personally written note. Thank-you letters from the people who will ultimately benefit from the contribution are the most effective because they usually contain more passion and give specific direct benefits to the contributor. If the people who write the thank-you notes happen to be under the age of eight it can be all the better for your organization. Thank-you drawings and notes written in crayons from kids can say more than a two-page, glowing letter by the executive director of your organization. But don't do one or the other, do both.

The power of a thank-you note cannot be underestimated. Once when we were meeting with a United Way director, we broached the subject of thank-you notes. I said I would not give to United Way again until I received a thank-you from the United Way. I explained to her that the United Way was the only organization that had never thanked me with a written thank you note—and an ad saying "thanks to you it's working" doesn't cut it. She then argued with me for more than 30 minutes about why the United Way could not afford to send thank-you notes to all its contributors. I asked if I increased my gift from past years, could I get a thank you? One of my partners, who was an active United Way volunteer, was about to scream "I'll send him a thank you!" As my partner knew, all this executive director had to do was go back to the office, write a simple thank you, put on a stamp and send it back to me. The total cost; about 50 cents. My gift level before I stopped giving was about $1,000 per year.

People, even people who are in the fundraising business, like to be thanked again and again—even if they say they don't need it. We may give because of our own benevolence, but we also want to know that the money was appreciated and important to the mission of the organization.

Thank-you notes are big business in the profit world. However, here again, some think they are not necessary.

Mike Veeck, who owns major league baseball teams, said he writes 900 letters to season ticket holders. He has a 98 percent renewal. The letters are simple thank-you notes and a request to buy season tickets next year. You can't argue with the result.

And may I say again and again, thank you for investing in this book and for reading it.

What Ever Happened to Direct Delivery?

If you ask people what is the best way to get a message to a targeted audience, most people will begin with the mass media and then recommend the Internet. But, when you need to hit highly targeted audiences, one of the best ways is an old marketing idea—home delivery.

There was a day when you would get many materials delivered directly to your door. There is no reason why this technique won't work today. In fact, it just might work better because of the hyper-market world in which we live and that few people use this technique.

Door-hangers are new again. The average size is 4 inches by 9 inches with a hole cut out (die-cut) and a slit cut for ease of placing the card stock on doors. Many printers now have die-cuts ready for door hangers which helps bring down your costs. The door hangers are great for delivering a message to a home, but, if you really want to be remembered, clip a magnet on the door hanger. People still have refrigerators and kids still make works of art that need to be displayed.

The difficulty with door hangers is twofold: First, you must research your market by street to see where you want to deliver these vintage marketing gems; and second, you will need to find some foot-soldiers who will deliver the door hangers.

One of our clients used a few Boy Scouts to deliver the door hangers. These young teenage boys look unassuming and all-American. That means that most people were friendly as the boys went about their work hanging the advertising. If you really need a lot of feet on the pavement and you don't want to chaperon some teenagers, you may try some of the employment services or ask members of your staff who may want to earn some extra money on weekends. Make sure you spot-check to see that the deliveries were made and in a timely fashion.

Advertising

"Many a small thing has been made large by the right kind of advertising."
Mark Twain

Advertising Plan

Advertising by nonprofits sends a lot of mission-driven organizations into a tizzy. According to a *BusinessWeek* article titled, "Selling a Cause? Better Make It Pop," "With competition fierce, charities are finding that savvy marketing is a must," trusted charities are using ad-campaigns to stake ground in the fundraising and awareness wars.

What has happened? A lot. Do you see many Public Service Ads (PSAs) on television? Maybe at Midnight or later. All media, from the networks to local billboard companies, are inundated with requests for free time. National organizations such as the Ad Council ($1 million entry fee for organizations) and the American Heart Association (who spent $1.5 million over two years) are taking up more and more of the content placements. Many stations run their own public service efforts (and sell sponsorship to them), which also limits the PSA-availability pool.

It is estimated that there are more than 1 million nonprofit organizations in the US. What can a local effort do? Do what some of the national charities have started to do—pay for advertising. I know this doesn't sound right. But let me tell you a story about the Iowa Donor Network.

The Iowa Donor Network (IDN) operates as the primary contact for organ tissue and eye donation services in the state of Iowa. They are a statewide agency that had little name recognition and a need to begin an online registry for people to indicate their willingness to be organ donors. The IDN pulled together $300,000 for a statewide media campaign. Considering that many retailers spend more than that in one market in a year, this was a tall order.

Because of our small budget (in relation to the task), to reach the entire state we focused all the money into one medium. But then, we focused even more: We asked television stations to compete for 100 percent of the buy in the five television markets. Many of the stations came to the table with wonderful proposals which made the IDN a station project. Others just brought a list of advertising avails (time you could buy and the price) and a promise for "value-added." We selected one station in each market. Yes, there was some mild fallout as the losing stations blustered about a bit, but the plan was sound.

The results were what quieted the critics. The IDN was able to actually receive more than $600,000 in advertising value as a result of the buy. Several stations ran news stories featuring the Iowa Donor Registry during donation month and one station ran a 30-minute program on organ donation right after the 6:00 pm news as part of the package. The moral of the story: as a mission-driven organization, if you bring some money to the table, most media outlets will do everything they can to give you extra advertising because of your service status. In other words, when all the other organizations are begging, you bring value to the negotiation table. That is a win-win.

When you do advertise you run the risk of looking too business-like. This may turn off contributors, so make sure your ads focus on the people you serve and not become a brag-fest about your organization.

It is funny, when I told this story to another organization that is very similar to the size and scope of the IDN, the response was, "we can't do that, we have to spread the money around to all the media. They are our friends." The media are not your friends. They are selling machines that are no different than a Wal-Mart or a Target.

Loud and Literal

There is no getting around it: today the myriad media outlets and opportunities for sales messages are overwhelming. It's estimated you receive 3,000 messages per day. Just 30 years ago it was around 500 messages a day. For any advertiser there is a real need to be "loud and literal" when delivering a message. But the message also needs to be consistent to achieve the desired results. Frequency is the secret ingredient to your success. It is estimated that adults must hear a message at least seven times before it settles into long-term memory. You have to tell them, tell them and tell them again to see results.

Imagine swinging a golf club correctly one time and then expecting to play well every time you hit the links. You need to correctly swing consistently, and with enough frequency to brand the swing into your muscles and mind.

I like to call it "frequent consistency." You need your message—the right message for the audience—delivered again and again. That means an integrated message through all your potential touches with your audience: letters, thank-you notes, brochures, Web sites, and advertising.

It is Time to Budget Advertising

This is the hardest part of any marketing plan: determining what you should spend to be successful. Many companies use between 3 to 7 percent of sales to determine their advertising budgets. So, if your annual revenue is $2 million, you should be allocating approximately $60,000 to marketing your organization. Think of an advertising budget as being like the federal government's education budget. It is difficult to estimate exactly what we need to do the job right, so we establish ratios to help us. For example, the federal government uses a percent of Gross National Product to determine the budget, and Congress then decides each year if it should go up or down from that number.

If this is your first year for a true advertising budget, then you will be off the target. You will need to make adjustments in year two depending on share of voice, competitor marketing efforts, your total budget and the local economy—and the comfort of your board with a marketing campaign.

If you don't have a marketing director, don't hire one as part of this investment. You need to save the money to work the media, not plan the campaign.

The Research Question

"Ready. Fire. Aim."
Anonymous

U nfortunately, research is just not part of many organizations' strategic plans. You may have conducted a feasibility study as part of a capital campaign, but most organizations do little in the way of market research. It is all anecdotal.

Most organizations would like to increase awareness in a marketplace. However without a baseline how do they know if the awareness has increased or decreased? A survey that will measure your baseline will probably cost $15,000 to $20,000. That is too much for most organizations to spend on measuring awareness. Yet, before you hire that marketing director, you have to ask what is that person going to do and how are you going to measure that person's effectiveness. Do the research first otherwise it is "ready, fire, aim."

At a minimum, you should regularly survey your mailing list: First, people will appreciate that you are trying to improve your service; second, you will learn valuable information from your efforts.

Survey your stakeholders either with a written survey or develop an online component. Your survey may not be statistically valid, but you will gain valuable information about what your stakeholders are really thinking.

The trend in business is that only one question really matters: "Would you recommend us to a friend?" Of course there is also a follow-up question of "Why or why not?" It seems that question is also relevant to all mission-driven organizations.

Some of the key questions you may want to also ask are as follows:

1) *How well do you feel Org X has communicated its mission? Rank 1-10*
2) *How well do you feel you know what Org X does for our community? Rank 1-10*
3) *How could Org X improve its communications with you? What do you want to know?*
4) *Would you recommend Org X to a friend? Why or why not?*
5) *When you talk with friends, how well do they know Org X's mission and vision? Rate 1-10*

Keeping the survey simple and short will allow you to easily tabulate answers. The difficult step will be keeping the survey consistent from quarter to quarter or year to year so you can benchmark and measure progress on various issues.

Broadcast Television

M uch has been written about the demise of television as an advertising medium. It is usually written in a newspaper or magazine so you must really question the source. Newspapers love to slam television. Yet one of the most popular newspaper areas is the TV section of the paper: newspapers constantly report on television stars, and many are toying with "television-like" sections on their Web sites. In spite of this obvious love affair with television, reporters continue to paint television as some monolithic force. For most people, television is not one thing, but many channels, many stations. You probably have a favorite local network-affiliated television station for news.

Sure, television's audience shares (a share point will be defined later in this chapter) have decreased. But local television is still a powerful medium, and you may be able to afford local television.

Television allows you to tell your story visually, verbally and musically, all at the same time. This combination is powerful, and it may be the most effective medium to date. I worked in television for 15 years at a local NBC affiliate. I learned of the branding power that only television can make happen. Imagine how the AFLAC "duck" campaign would have worked if it were a newspaper campaign. Another important element in television is its ability to give an organization instant credibility in the marketplace, just by being on TV.

Television allows you to "show" people what your organization can accomplish. Think of the phrase, "Seeing is believing." People can literally see the kinds of services you deliver every day.

The number-one disadvantage of television commercials is not clutter, decreased shares or higher cost per points (the cost per rating point which is a percentage of the television audience, 1 point = 1 % of the audience in a given market). What really hurts television's effectiveness is that people try to say too much in 30 seconds. The difference between national and local ads usually is in the sophistication of the message: national ads usually have only one point per ad, local commercials tend to try and cram in as many copy points as possible.

Another positive point of television is that many people multi-task while they are watching television. (In fact I'm writing this chapter while watching the Super Bowl's pre-game show.) One of the common multi-tasks is surfing the Internet. So, television makes an excellent medium to point people to your Web site.

Where to Advertise on Television?

There is a lot of talk about diminishing audiences on television. This is true; however television continues to be a dominating medium with large audiences especially for people older than 35. One program category that is not being hurt by TiVo or competition from other networks is local news.

In our market, the three main broadcast affiliates that offer local news command a 60 share of audience—or, 60 percent of all the viewers watching at 6:00 pm. What that means is that nearly 150,000 people in our television market will see your ad if you bought one spot on each of the three stations.

If you do venture into the world of buying local television to support your cause, it will take a budget of $15,000 to $20,000, in medium to smaller markets, to make any kind of difference. If your budget is small, one way to have an impact on television is to *own* a program. In other words, instead of sprinkling your television money around the television day, it is actually more effective to focus the money and provide a more concentrated effort on a particular day-part. If you do so, you'll still receive the results—high reach and frequency numbers.

For example, in the Cedar Rapids-Waterloo-Dubuque television market, our marketing firm will often recommend owning Sunday night 10:00 pm news. This time period has the same large audience as other nights and is priced lower than other newscasts. Remember, television is priced by the amount of audience and demand. There is a high audience on Sunday but low demand.

Recently we prepared a buy that reached 98 percent (that is called reach) of the male population ages 35 and older over the course of one year. The commercial would be seen an average of four to five times by the audience (that is frequency). You can receive a reach and frequency report on any buy you make with a television station. You will see reach (the number of nonduplicated people who will see the commercial) and frequency (the number of times each person will see the commercial).

What to say?

For most organizations this is the rub. What do you say about all the great things you do for a community? One of the best uses of television would be to drive home that you have sent out a mailing.

If you have a mailing dropping on December 3, I would suggest running a campaign from December 1 through December 8. This week-long campaign's goal is to boost response on that mailing. For less than $5,000 (and some production costs) in a medium-sized market you should be able to buy eight to ten news spots during that week. The television stations might even match your buy because you are a 501c3 organization raising your reach and frequency during that short burst.

The message would be your annual theme, plus benefits about giving to your organization. Showing the appeal on the air will help people identify your mailing among the onslaught of appeal letters during that time of year. So, your one message should be "When you see this blue envelope, please make a gift and light up a child's Christmas."

This spot will do some branding, but, for the most part, you are only trying to increase giving from non-givers and people who are not regular givers to your annual campaigns.

Big Message, Big Audience

B ecause I worked in television so long, some people accuse me of not being "outdoor-friendly." It's not that I don't like billboards, it's just that I don't recommend outdoor unless it will really fit the need.

In other words, those in the billboard industry would say I don't push billboards. I think one of the most effective forms of advertising is a billboard on a highway that says McDonalds Next Exit. But you need to use billboards the way they are intended to be used: use very few words, a large image and a logo. You can't say much more. One face is stronger than two. Two words make the most effective copy. Seven words are the absolute maximum you can read driving by a billboard.

Don't get caught up in the sales game—which medium pulls better than another. The problem is that they all work when used appropriately and with the right message.

When you want a "larger than life" appearance or message, then there is nothing better than outdoor to deliver. Billboards are especially vivid when you use the "rotary-sized" billboards and flex-vinyl covering. The colors are vibrant and clear. Photographs look great. The flex-vinyl can be used for several years (depending on weather). However there is a charge for the flex-vinyl.

A lot is changing in the outdoor-market arena: there are bus wraps (where the entire bus is covered with a billboard); car and van wraps; ads on cabs, building wraps, signs next to bus stops, and bus-stop bench ads.

One of the most exciting breakthroughs in outdoor is the digital billboard. I saw one of the test sites when vacationing in Destin, Florida. Most billboards charge for location. With the digital billboards you can now place location and time. While we sat at a stoplight, more than five billboards were "broadcast" on a screen the size of a rotary billboard. Simple dissolves between the boards still gave the feeling of motion so your eye was attracted to each change. Because of the accident potential I don't see any commercials being used on the boards, but there could be a movement to try them since we've not had the chance to experiment yet. The ability to target your message to audiences at different times has huge potential for all advertisers.

Direct Mail

M any people have predicted the demise of direct mail with the advent of the Internet. I don't know about your mailbox, but mine is full every day with catalogs, letters, invoices, investment notices, cards from friends, postcards from businesses, and packages from Internet purchases. The box is stuffed. There is a true art and science to direct mail. Many thought the Internet would have eliminated direct mail.

No medium has ever eradicated the previous medium. Newspapers didn't kill speeches; radio didn't kill newspapers; TV didn't kill radio; cable didn't kill broadcast TV; and the Internet will not kill direct mail. I still contend that I would rather receive a nice, hand-written thank-you more than an e-mail thank-you. It is just not the same to receive an e-mail birthday card in place of one's relatives sending a card in the mail. The look and feel of leafing through a catalog on the couch compared to searching a Web site on your computer is the same as the difference between McDonalds and Starbucks coffees.

However, frequency of message is key for direct mail just as it is in other media. Have you ever ordered something from a catalog that you've seen many times before but had thrown out the earlier catalogs? We all have. That is why frequency works. It may seem like a simple concept, but this critical detail evades many marketers: Long-term, consistent messages have a cumulative effect over time. So, you must begin a steady diet of messages to your targeted audiences. That is why we are so against the quarterly newsletter. It does not provide enough frequency to make a difference.

Direct mail can come in many shapes and sizes. A mixture of postcards and mini-brochures is what will probably work best for your organization. I would prefer you to do more simple mailings rather than fewer, but more elaborate mailings.

The Key to Direct Mail

The key to any good direct mail effort is the quality of your list. Many organizations have been mailing newsletters to a list that no one has really researched in years. The cost of printing and postage keep going up as the number of names keeps growing. Few people ever come off the list.

There are a number of good fundraising databases that will help in this process. These software packages can be expensive, but they are worth their weight in gold in maintaining a good mailing database (and will probably save you money in the end because they will eliminate people from your mailing lists).

A good list manager should update names, but also code the names for connections to the organization such as contributors, friends, volunteers, and employees. If you don't have these coded now, though it is an arduous task, it must be done before you send out another mailing.

Make sure that your mailing list includes VIPs in your area. Occasionally chambers of commerce will maintain a list like this that you can buy, but for the most part, you will need to build this list yourself. This list should include presidents and CEOs of major companies, politicians and chamber board members. You should also include potential board members for your organization. These people can be identified in the newspaper when they are featured serving on other boards of directors. These people may not understand why they are getting your information at first, but when you call on them to serve they will have a level of familiarity that will help land them.

Direct Mail Returns

There is much written about rates of return for direct-mail efforts. Depending on the quality of your list, your returns will probably be much better than what we have described here. By adding television to the mix or e-mailing people to watch for your mailing, you will increase your rates of return. You should track the timing and rates of return on all your mailings so you know which mailings were the most successful.

Direct Mail Return Expectations Estimation

Year	Mailing	Return .25%	Return .5%	Return 1%
I	15,000	38	75	150
II	25,000	63	125	250

The year II example shows you've increased your mailing by 10,000. Let's say you bought a list of likely givers in your market area. Because you advertised the mailing you achieved a 1 percent rate of return. That is 250 people. If your average gift is $100 from that group you have returned $25,000 from the mailing. If you only achieve a $50 average gift and .5 percent return, the total is $6,250—only enough to cover the mailing costs and printing.

Creative/Getting Noticed

There are plenty of great direct mail ideas. The problem is that the more complicated the mailing, the greater the cost. We've used letters, postcards with Web, and Lenticular designs. The last one is an old technique utilizing a 3-D look which is now less expensive. As you tilt the image, it changes. For example a Coke bottle starts full and, as you tilt the card, it shows the bottle emptying. Mailers have also tried boxes with little toys, and pillow-like see-through packages. You name it, it has been mailed.

To be a success you must tell a compelling story, one that will resonate with your stakeholders and motivate them to action. Find good stories that show your proof of performance. You say you "do good," then tell us about a real person who has benefited.

Postage Stamps

There is one other little technique that could cause a big buzz in your organization's mail efforts. The US Post Office will accept stamps with photos on them. At Stamp.com you can get almost any photograph printed as official postage on an adhesive sticker. They will not accept any offensive photos. The PhotoStamps come in sheets of 20. They are not cheap. The stamps cost from 30 to 50 cents more than the face value of the postage. There are volume discounts. For those hard to impress top contributors, a picture may be worth a thousand words.

Radio Advertising

Radio is really going through a major transition. First, there was rapid growth of stations in nearly every market. Then, there was the consolidation of ownership, and now satellite radio may really shake things up. As well, now there are Pod-casts, iPods and MP3 players. Of all of these, I think when I heard my first satellite radio I was hooked.

Despite all the issues, radio is still a good medium to share stories and information in an economical format. Radio has many advantages, but, for most, the best part is its relative low cost. While in television advertising you can show things, the key to radio is repetition. During a radio commercial, you must repeat your name several times, and in a broadcast day, run your commercial many times within the schedule.

Even though radio units are sold in 30- and 60-second units for the same costs, it is recommended that you only run a 30. Sixty seconds of straight copy is too much to take, unless you have a compelling story to tell. Remember the principle of "one idea per commercial?" We'll, it is very hard to drag out one idea for 60 seconds. An exception may be car dealers who seem to think that is okay.

Radio is also a great medium for testimonials. Radio production allows you to heavily edit sound bites. This allows you to take the best from someone's interview.

Newspaper Advertising

Newspapers can be powerful advertising vehicles, but they are the most abused from a production standpoint. People try to put too much into an ad thinking they are paying for every square inch so they will fill every square inch.

Unfortunately, fighting for attention is even more important in a newspaper ad. Unlike radio and television, people do not have to read your ad. So, you must reach out and grab attention. One way we have found to do this that is highly effective is to use page-dominant ads instead of full-page ads. These page-dominant ads are tall enough to go over the fold and wide enough to force out any other advertising. Usually page-dominant ads are surrounded by a news story, because the ad fills most of the typical size people buy for newspaper ads. For example: if a newspaper is 6 columns wide, a page dominant ad would be 5 columns wide and 13 to 14 inches tall. The real advantage is that the page-dominant ad costs less than the full-page ad but has all the advertising punch.

The other secret to powerful newspaper advertising is "white space." This takes an enormous amount of advertising discipline to accomplish, but the appearance of a lot of white space in a sea of newspaper gray visually draws a reader's eye to the ad.

Newspapers are also looking for new ways to increase revenue and fight off any leakage to the Internet. In a sea of squares and rectangles, some newspapers are accepting innovative shapes to help boost ad effectiveness. Some triangle shapes are making it onto pages and even ads with no straight-line borders, which are blended into content, are being tested in Dallas and Chicago. However don't expect these unique ad formats to hit your local papers soon, but they surely will be part of newspapers in the future.

Internet Marketing

"One of the Internet's strengths is its ability to help consumers find the
right needle in a digital haystack of data."
Brian Tracy

Web Site Marketing

The Web is a powerful tool for reaching your market. Many people will check out a Web site just to see what your organization is all about.

One of the most important things for the Web site to do is to motivate action. Few mission-driven organizations realize that your Web site needs an action goal. Ask what do you want people to do as result of visiting your Web site? Is it to volunteer or donate or advocate? Web sites cost too much to build and maintain to just educate the public.

The ultimate goal is to get a Web site visitor on to a more personalized sales process as soon as possible.

Web sites must accomplish these few critical goals: usability, visual attractiveness, persuasiveness, and interactivity. Of all these goals, interactivity or the appearance of interactivity is critical to a given Web site's success. To achieve this balance Web sites require a holistic approach, encompassing many disciplines.

A Little Web Marketing Background

The Web is a truly wonderful medium. However it is not television, and not exactly like brochures, newspapers, or radio. It is its own medium, filled with its own idiosyncrasies and uses.

The problem is that people want to make a Web site something it is not. It certainly is not a static environment. Even though the Internet was created 20 years ago, it is still a relatively new medium. We are learning new ways to use the Web every day, and the Web is evolving as we learn.

A Few Basics about the Web

The Internet is probably one of the most talked-about and most researched areas of business. After working with clients at the macro level, a few theories of Web development have become apparent to me. As in any page design, the Web has its areas of importance in regard to the screen. Generally, if you draw an X on your screen, the area slightly above true-center is the most important spot on your Web page. It is called *visual center*. The viewer's eye is naturally drawn to that spot, so make sure it holds something special for people to see.

Web Site Eye-flow Analysis

Another important consideration is eye-flow across the page. Web site eye-flow is generally thought to start in the upper left hand corner and then in a circular movement begin to loop across the page ending on the lower left hand side. Notice that on most Web sites, this is where most navigation bars are placed. Though not a hard and fast rule, it does give a Web page builder a guide for placing information of high importance.

Notice we did not say, "And then the person scrolls to see what is below on the page." Scrolling should be avoided. Studies show that the majority of visitors will skip a page rather than scroll through a long area.

Navigability, usability and accessibility are words people like to throw around when talking about the Web. They are important, but first, people must go to your site and then they must be persuaded to stay.

Most sites can be called "Scan" sites. This means that these sites are more likely to be scanned by the target audience—especially early in the process. So, you must be quick and efficient at telling people what you want them to know, and, most importantly what you want them to do. Only then will people be pulled more deeply into your site.

Upgrade the Web Site to a Sales Site

The goal of your site cannot be to educate. You will spend too many resources and too much staff time trying to create an educational site. The site must *motivate*.

So the first thing you must do is establish one central goal for your Web site. For most of you it will be fundraising. Once that goal is accomplished, you can then use your fundraising goal as a filter through which you run all other ideas. This will help in the prioritization of key areas. You must do this, because unlike a brochure, the Web has no limits. You can put as much information on your site as you like.

If your Web site is a fundraising site, then the home page must begin the sales process. One way to help people understand the value of a gift is to create a calculator page. This allows people to have some interactivity with your site. For example, potential contributors could select from an area of interest, say children's services. Next they enter the dollar amount they are considering contributing and, the calculator then shows what can happen in children's services at that gift level. You could even show a "community betterment index" that would show the community improving with each gift.

You can put on the site the cost of fundraising or a breakdown of how efficient you are with contributed dollars and other revenue. This "dollarizing" of your effort will help people understand how frugal you are with their contributed dollars and how efficient you are with your service delivery.

You know that, if people can enter dollar amounts, they will experiment with different levels of giving. As the dollars go up more people are helped, more needed items are purchased and the community is helped more.

We need that kind of matrix to have an equal effect, but it will also need to have disclaimers, and you will need a strong statement that this calculator is for demonstration purposes only. The real benefit is that this kind of calculator allows people to play and interact with your Web site.

Here are ideas to improve your Web site and begin to really sell over the Internet:

- Humanize the look of the site. Almost every mission-driven organization is a people agency. Show a lot of people on your site. Research shows that people looking directly out from ads pulls more than ads without people.
- Testimonials. Web sites are a great place to feature testimonials. Let your testimonials tell your story rather than long copy. If you can find the people, have a testimonial for each service area on your site. You can have the testimonials change as the user clicks from page to page.
- Have a professional work on your site. I have visited many sites; many look like "Web amateur hour." I know we want to look like we have not been extravagant; the problem is that communications is lost when the site looks like your Uncle Charlie designed it. Also, a kid who just graduated from college cannot independently design a site for contributors. You need people who are contributors helping to make sure the site is relevant.
- Use IPIX photographs to show different buildings and services on your site. I'm sure you have seen this technique on hotel Web sites.

On these sites you can see a 360-degree wide-angle view of your room, from side to side and ceiling to floor. The secret is that the person viewing the page has control of the photo and can move it all around giving a great interactive feel to the page.

■ Create a "white paper" area on your site. Here you will place position papers that you generate on behalf of your organization. When people really want to go deeper into your organization they can do so in the comfort of their own homes. But, a word of warning: The position papers do need to take a position. People want meat in these "white papers" not a lot of bun. Using Top 10 concepts really works well with these kinds of papers and makes them easier to write (i.e. "The Top 10 Ways to Help Troubled Children in Our Community").

■ Make stars of your people. Most shy away from singling out people on Web sites because they might leave. Well, one way to give your employees more worth and a sense of real belonging is to create features on different employees on your site. You know that the employee will e-mail all of his or her friends and relatives. Who knows, you may be generating new contributors through this effort. The employees will love it, but also the potential contributors will feel that they better know the organization. This kind of effort breeds familiarity and that is the first step to a real connection.

■ Use videos on your Web site. At the least, a short introduction by your CEO should be part of the site. You can also show tours of buildings, listen to children's programs, watch counselors at work, and whatever else helps people "see" what you are doing to further your service. If you can, you can also make some Pod casts to be posted on iTunes. This will show people that you are a very progressive agency, even if they can't download or don't own an iPod.

■ Capitalize the real words of your URL (Uniform Resource Locator). The capital letters will not impact the navigation, and doing so will help them remember it and use it. Can you read this URL?

www.capitalizewordsinyoururl.org

Now try:

www.CapitalizeWordsInYourURL.org

We need capitalization to make sense. Even the most computer adroit teenager who text-messages and IMs will appreciate being able to read the URL, even if only at some subconscious level.

The two goals for your site should be a sales focus and interactivity. These are what will keep people coming back again and again. You want your Web site to create buzz, not look like everyone else's site. The Web can really be a point of distinction. Try to have your site be a Web "wow" moment.

Search Engine Optimization

Research shows that nearly 90 percent of Web surfers use search engines (such as Google and Yahoo!) to find new Web sites. This was once a free area of marketing, but alas, the free lunch is over and soon it may get worse.

It's not enough to have a good site; today you must make sure people can easily find it. Several companies are offering "pay-per-click" search services. With such a service, you buy key words and then pay per click for a search word or word grouping. This does make it difficult for a very local organization, because many of the best words are already taken or "bid up" by national businesses and organizations.

The cost usually is in the 10 to 80 cents per-click range. However, the more common the word (or the more competition in a category) the higher the price for the word or groups of words.

You pay a flat fee, for example $500. Then after 3,333 people click on your search words your account is depleted and you are out of money. The good news is that you know exactly what you are getting in advance; the bad news is that you don't know if it is someone in your office checking to see how high you come up on search engines. You do only pay for people who are looking for your specific search words. If you are a Red Cross agency you may want to buy "Iowa Red Cross" or the town you're in followed by Red Cross. Otherwise you will be bidding against every Red Cross for the listing.

There are many ways to raise the level of your site on search engines, but it is not an exact science. Needless to say, you must have someone dedicated to maintaining your site high on search lists.

Should You Be Blogging?

S ome view Web logs—or blogs—as "off-the-cuff ramblings" from techno-geeks with too much time on their hands. But the blogosphere is becoming more mainstream. Even General Motors has a blog which it used to quell rumors that it was eliminating the Pontiac and Buick brands.

Business Week estimated that there are 4.8 million blogs in existence. How is that for mainstream?

Blogs can provide a transparent unfiltered area where you can interact with your stakeholders. If you use it for public relations releases you are missing the point and your blog will become ignored.

Good blogs need access to specific people in your organization, information not available from other sources, and a little of the raw emotion found on the editorial pages of newspapers. Without the emotion, the blog is a bust. In a blog readers want your opinion, your thoughts and your predictions of the future.

You can start today posting your blog on any Web-logging service. Or you can set up a blog on your current Web site. It is as easy as that—except for the writing, of course. Once you start, you must continually add new postings. People can respond to your blog with questions and comments. Some of the responses may make you mad, but that is one risk in entering the blog world.

The second issue in blogging is getting people to read your blog. Again, as with your Web site, you need to let people know you have posted a new blog. If people have subscribed to your blog they will get it right away, but a pool of subscribers may take years to build. In the meantime, you will need to rely on e-mail, postcards and phone calls to get the word out.

You can bypass the written Web log and directly enter the vloggers realm of communicating. Vloggers are video bloggers. With a digital camera you can post a simple video message. You will find, however, that a telepromter (a way to read copy while still looking into the camera lens) will really come in very handy.

A blog or videoblog will really provide you with a forum to help your organization advocate for the people you serve. You can send e-mail updates to stakeholders, legislators, community leaders and the mainstream press when you have posted a new topic on the blog or vblog and the topic. It may be the springboard to getting people talking and buzzing about your organization and the issues facing it and the people you serve. There are some issues with downloading video blogs, so many people are going right to pod casting and personal video messages rather than vblogs.

Pod casting, and posting your pod cast on iTunes, have the potential to be a wonderful communications devices for mission-driven organizations. The only real problem is that many of your stakeholders and contributors probably are not in the demographic of persons who own iPods.

Virtual Open House

When you remodel your offices or build a new building you invite people over for a reception and ribbon-cutting. It's an open house and we've all done it. Yet, when you go through the extensive process of remodeling your Web site or building a new Web site there is little fanfare. In fact, I can't remember when I received any kind of acknowledgement that there was a newly remodeled site, except for notices on my invoices from different companies and that is not the environment for new sales.

Once your redesign is completed, let people know that you have remodeled your site and are open for business. Prepare a simple postcard inviting people to attend a virtual Open House at your Web address. List a specific time and day for the event. Then, mail the card to your targeted list of stakeholders. Don't forget local mayors, presidents of major industry, legislators and especially news reporters who will likely pick up on the virtual open-house concept.

If you want to do a "real" virtual open house, set up a way for people to register online in order to receive a free item. You would give away some food and beverages at a real open house, so why not a small gift for taking the time to register? Make sure you are collecting e-mail addresses.

The prize could be a free cup of coffee at Starbucks, Krispy Kreme donuts or sodas at a convenience store. By working an agreement with such an establishment, you could offer an Internet coupon. Or you could go to the expense of sending back a small prize.

You could also have a live chat during the open house or have people sign in on a registry that posts the people in real time. This would help add to the interactivity of your new site.

At the absolute minimum, you must send out a postcard announcing your new site. Too many times we assume that because we are open everyone knows or cares. Let people know—*beat your gong*—and give people real benefits for attending your virtual open house—*and then you'll sell your candies*.

Publications

"However far your travels take you, you will never find the girl who smiles out at you from the travel brochure."
Anonymous

Integrated Marketing

Integrated marketing is a fancy phrase that means, "Does your marketing all look alike? Is it delivering the same look, same feel, and same message?" This is important especially when you have a small budget. With limited resources you can't afford to let a message go by without people knowing who it is from and what the message is. It is more than color, more than design, more than words. It is all of these combined.

Here is an easy test. Take all of your publications, photos of your signs and billboards, letterhead, business cards, newsletters and fan them out on your desk. Step back and look at the collection. Does this grouping of publications look like it came from the same organization? Does the font match from piece to piece? Does the color match? Bring in some people from the outside to assess what you've fanned out. Also, look at anything that stands out from the grouping.

Integrated marketing takes advantage of the cumulative effect of marketing. Each piece seems to have greater returns because it is combined with the message from a previous piece. It is a problem if the pieces look and feel different: then there is no cumulative effect.

Nike can afford to look different from ad to ad, but if you do the same comparison with Nike's materials, you will quickly see a look consistency, a consistent feel in the design and copy and an integrated marketing approach that works.

Cancel Your Newsletter Today

I get newsletters from a number of mission-driven organizations and a few things always strike me as odd. For one, where is the *news* and where is the conversational *letter*-style of writing? Get it? News-letter. There is a reason a newsletter is so named, yet few seem to grasp the importance of the words used. In the 25 or so years I've been working with marketing, the newsletter just doesn't seem to change: I continue to see outdated, boring articles, a bland (and extremely safe) letter from the CEO, a couple of bad photographs from an event or two, a smattering of bragging articles, a "look who is new" section, a complete disclaimer (not required but copied from every other publication) including listings of all the people who worked so hard on the newsletter, and a message from the fundraising department. In your newsletter, I'm sure once a year you cram in the names of contributors to make sure they are appropriately thanked. Does that sum up your publication? One mission-focused group I worked with spent more than $40,000 on four newsletters a year. For this cash-strapped organization this outlay was a treasure-trove of funds they could use to begin a real marketing effort to their stakeholders.

The first step is to cancel your newsletter. You need to make a commitment to this process or it just won't work. Canceling will help you through the next steps. Until you formally abandon it you will not be able to think outside the newsletter box. When a hospital we worked with canceled its newsletter, not one person called or wrote to ask what happened. A few of the hospital's department heads asked, because they wanted to put some information in it, but it disappeared without a reader complaint.

Once you've committed yourself to breakthrough thinking, now ask yourself these simple questions:

1. *Who do we need to talk to?*
2. *Put the audiences into a priority list: who is most important, who is second etc.*
3. *What do I want to tell people about my organization?*
4. *What do I need to tell people? These can't be the same thing.*
5. *What do people want to know about my organization?*
6. *What do we have to say that is interesting to our target audience? Notice I did not say "audiences."*

The last question is the key to your future marketing. Most of what goes into newsletters is internal information, chocked-full of internal jargon-speak. Here is the first inherent problem with newsletters: they are not targeted. This is your first clue that your publication will be ineffective if you say you are trying to hit multiple audiences with one message.

Now that you've canceled your newsletter, analyzed what it is you really need to say, and to whom you should say it, it is time to address the marketing vehicle you should use.

I would suggest a 6-inch X 9-inch postcard to start. This size will force you to keep the writing crisp and factoid-like so that it is a quick read. Have some nice photographs. Since you are only going to have a few photos you can spend some money to make sure they are professional and communicate the right message.

The postcards will cost less to print and mail so you will be able to dramatically increase the frequency and immediacy of information. Postcards are more likely to be read because they don't have an envelope and are not sealed in any way.

Of course, you are probably thinking of making an e-mail format of the same information. I would agree, except that most organizations have a small e-mail list of people to communicate with. Postcards deliver a short, highly-targeted message, but it is not just one postcard that has the impact. The secret to success of this approach is in the cumulative effect of receiving 12 to 15 postcards per year. The quarterly newsletter allows too much time to transpire between communications. The postcard allows for a monthly or twice-monthly communications. The impact will be dramatic in audience perception of the organization and in proof of your performance over the year.

Start Your Publications with Benefits, Not Attributes

Take a close look at your general brochure. Does it start with the, "Org X is a nonprofit, 501C3 organization?" If it is does, you have lost your audience. By starting with the attributes of your organization you become just another struggling, begging organization. Instead, start with power. "Org X rebuilds poor people's lives." Starting with your benefits is loud and literal. It helps people know exactly what you do and why they should support you.

We've already talked about benefits and the power they have to persuade. Have you heard the phrase, "You never get a second chance to make a first impression?" It is true when you first meet someone and when you start to read a brochure. Many organizations worry about the wording for accuracy, yet don't take a minute to make sure that the benefits to the reader are front and center in the publication. Start with your headlines. Do they pop with the power of benefits? Then work on the body copy. This is art, not science. So pay close attention to how these words will impact your target audience, not the people down the hall. Review all your publications tomorrow. Collect everything you have published and spread it out on a large table and begin to read the headlines and body copy. Analyze what really is working and what is not.

Power of Letters

The more technology finds its way into our lives, the more powerful personal communications become. When was the last time you received a hand-written letter? Today, so many of us have access to word-processing that even personal letters are typed, formatted, and laser-printed.

Here's an idea to bring personalization and the personal touch home to your key stakeholders. For your next campaign, hire a group of teenage girls to handwrite letters for you. I'm not trying to get you in an employment discrimination suit, but girls have much better penmanship so avoid boys unless you know they have excellent writing skills. Hire the girls for two days and pay them $7 per hour. That's $56 dollars for eight hours of work. Each girl should be able to write 10 to 20 letters per hour—especially if you keep the letters short. That's about 100 letters per day. Five girls would produce a total of 1,500 hand-written letters in three days work, at a cost of $168. Don't forget to have the girls write the addresses on the envelopes.

The point to this approach is that the letter is highly personalized with the amount the person gave last year. There is also a clear call to action by asking for double the amount that was given last year, though you could ask for 20 percent more, 10 percent more, or whatever meets your goals.

On the contribution card you include in the packet, you should not have typical gift totals. Just include a line on which the person can fill in the amount. Hand-write last year's contribution number in a space provided on the card. This will put added pressure on the person to increase giving. If the person didn't give last year, don't write zero, just leave it blank. The recipient will get the message. Have the name and address hand-written on the contribution card as well.

For example:

Dear Mr. and Mrs. Smith
111 South St.
Iowa City, Iowa 55555

Dear Bill and Liz:

Thank you for your gift to Waypoint last year of $100. And thank you for your support over the past few years.

Your $100 gift allowed a battered wife and her children to be sheltered—safe from violence—for one month. Your contribution really made a difference in the lives of a vulnerable and fragile family.

This year Bill and Liz, the need is even greater. More shattered families are in need. If you can find it in your heart, please consider doubling your gift this year. It will more than double the impact on the children who are so needy especially this time of year.

Again, thank you for your past support. We look forward to hearing from you again. Please don't hesitate to call.

Yours in the service to shattered families,

Sally Thompson
President, Waypoint

PS: You really do make a difference in the lives of women and children. I can assure you that your gift will go directly to helping people who need it most.

Personalization

I'm always struck by the lack of personalization in today's highly electronic and digital world. Personalization is just a long word meaning use my name. I still receive letters made out to Dear Friend. I get postcards that seem like the organization doesn't have a clue who I am or what I've done.

Today, because of strides in digital printing, you can personalize a postcard to each person you're mailing. In fact, you can personalize all the copy throughout the brochure with the person's name. The headline can have a name. The call-to-action at the end can have a name ("Bill, please give so that kids will live"). With all the clutter, nothing stands out more than a person's name.

If your organization can't afford to personalize the materials, then personalize the message. That means using the writing style of focusing your postcard, direct mailing or letter to one person. Use the word "you" throughout the letter which will help put the emphasis on one person. Remember, you are not writing to a group of people, you are writing to one person who happens to be in a group or list you constructed. I know you can do it.

Too Many Brochures

L ook around your office. How many brochures does you organization have? At most meetings I've attended the brochure is the equivalent of a Band-Aid: No one knows we do that, then, let's do a brochure: not enough people understand what we do, let's do a brochure; we are out of toilet paper, let's do a brochure.

There is nothing wrong with brochures. However, they are a microcosm of the real issue facing marketers—too much clutter.

Brochures are a medium just like television, radio or billboards. Some brochures break through the clutter others fade into the buzz. The first step is to narrow the focus. It seems that too many brochures try to accomplish too many goals. Brochures that are designed as general information, fundraising and specific project brochures—all in one—are doomed to failure. Target the audience first. Then design a brochure just for that audience: What do they want to know?

Brochure Focus Exercise
Fill this out when you want to do a new brochure

Target Audience for Brochure:

_____

_____

_____

What are the key points you want this audience to know?
1)_____ 2)_____
_____3)_____
____4)_____ 5)_____
_____6)_____

What are the benefits (not attributes) of this information to the key audience?

_____
_____
_____

What in this brochure needs to be different because of the target audience? (For example: a brochure for seniors needs large type)

_____
_____
_____

How will we deliver the brochure to the key audience?

_____
_____
_____

What will make this brochure stand out in the eyes of our target audience?

_____
_____
_____

The last two questions are critical: Everyone loves to talk about tactics, and a brochure is an easy tactical fix. But the real problem is delivery. The question is not what do we want to say, but how will we get the message to the people we want to reach (and who are those people?). There are thousands of brochures sitting in boxes (some may be sitting in your office as you read this) collecting dust. If they are that good, get them into the hands of the target audience. What is the reason to wait?

Think of your brochure as a medium, ready to sell today. If it can't live up to that, don't do the brochure.

Public Relations

*"Three hostile newspapers
are more to be feared than a thousand bayonets."*
Napoleon

Public Relations and
Your Organization

P ublic relations and media relations have been going on for a long, long time. Even Napoleon struggled with the press. The pen really is mightier than the sword.

But, for all mission-driven organizations, public relations is critically important. It may be the only time an organization's name gets any advertising at all is through public relations. The good news is that the "press" is growing: there are more media outlets today than at any time in the past. The explosion of blogs (Web Logs) and bloggers (Web log writers) plus the ability to create a "news station" or news outlet on the Web is creating more and more need to control your message and for you to perform well in front of all the press.

It is important to be press-prepared. The press is preparing for you. In journalism schools all over the country, aspiring journalists are learning about the first amendment to the Constitution, how to dig for stories, sourcing, and other tools in their story-finding and story-telling tool-box.

Before we go much farther, we must understand what news is. There seems to be a wealth of definitions about what news is and how it should be reported. Many think news outlets should only carry positive news while others think news should only be delivered with a certain political slant. Many mission-driven organizations operate in smaller markets that have local stations and newspapers that carry your news. The reporters are mostly young, energetic, but naive and ignorant when it comes to most issues facing mission-driven organizations today. Many of these reporters have no clue what a bond-issue is, how Medicare works, what the juvenile justice system is; they don't own homes, pay property taxes or join organizational boards. Most are very skeptical, because they have been told lies, hype, self-serving "goop" and muck from every politician, community leader and mission-driven organization in town.

All reporters are on deadlines that only fry-cooks can compare notes with. Television especially is deadline-brutal: news in the morning, noon, 5:00, 6:00 and 10:00 pm (CST). Newsrooms are chaotic—computers have quieted most newsrooms—but the pace prior to deadline gets things heated up.

Just imagine walking into work each day wondering if you will find the news of the day, or if you will you get "scooped" by myriad competitors? Information is bombarding the newsroom from faxes, e-mails, phone calls and press-releases. Most end up in the trash; most should go in the trash. What sorts to the top becomes the news of the day.

So what is news? My definition includes just one word: change. Something is not the same so it is news—things have improved, things have gotten worse, someone is instantly rich, someone has lost it all, happy neighbors are now warring, enemies are now working together. It is change. Now, if the change is unusual, includes a prominent person, is impactful, includes lots of money, or includes conflict, then it is definitely news.

The problem is that a lot of what people send out in press releases is neither change nor something new. It is the same thing repackaged. Your annual kickoff fundraising drive is a good example.

Think of your neighbors, what would be news to them. What could you do that would have people saying the next day, "Did you see that story about X last night?" That is news and that is great PR.

Being Press-Prepared

You can pretty much undo all the good marketing efforts you have done to date with a bad PR story. So PR is a critical part of the marketing tool-box. Public relations book after public relations book will tell you hundreds of ways to get publicity, stay in touch with reporters and write press releases. It is more likely, at many points in your career, you will be interviewed by the press. Most interviewees are just not prepared.

Here are 10 key points to help you be more prepared at your next encounter with the press. And remember, the press is everywhere. Bloggers can be in your audience typing, even as you are speaking at your next press conference.

Have you stopped beating your spouse?

There is no right answer to this question. Many organizations I work with complain about the questions reporters ask. We have a saying that there are no stupid questions, just stupid people who answer them. And it is true. A reporter can ask anything. However what is reported is not the question, but the answer. Don't get hung out to dry by paying too close attention to the question: instead focus on your answer.

If you are thrown a question you're just not ready for ask the reporter to repeat the question. This will give you some time to think of your answer. It may only be a few seconds, but it will feel like a lifetime if you are better able to formulate an effective answer. Another way to deal with a particularly tough question is to ask the reporter to rephrase the question. For example, you are asked, "Why does your organization discriminate against women?"

There is not a good answer to this question, none without risk of falling into a trap. So it is best to rephrase the question, "I think what you're asking is what can we do to avoid all discrimination?" Then answer your rephrased question.

Remember to stay on target with what you need and want to talk about. Sure you may complain that politicians don't answer the question asked, but can you blame them? How can politicians be experts on everything or know the answer to everything. They can't. But they can answer what they know about. A friend of mine was an Iowa representative. He said that no matter what he was asked, he would only talk about five areas. He used something we call the "15-10-15" rule for dealing with questions that he didn't have the answer to. He'd use the first 15 seconds to deal with the specific questions, 10 seconds to segue, and then the next 15 seconds to answer what "you really should know about." Here is how it might work.

Reporter: *Pat the state's economy is weak, exports are down and jobless benefits are up. How can we turn around Iowa's current economic situation?*

Pat: *I can really empathize with people who are out of work or underemployed, but you know what is really important is education, that is why I've outlined a five-point plan to improve the education in the state . . .*

Pat is not an expert on economic theories, but he is one on early childhood education. Similarly he is not an expert on energy policy, but he is on urban development.

The key is not the question, it is your answer. Think through what you need to say and answer accordingly.

Ignorance and Arrogance

There are really two reasons why many people do poorly when confronted by the press—they are ignorance and arrogance.

Let's start with *ignorance* because it gets many people into trouble when they don't realize what they are doing. Mostly people are friendly, and when they meet a reporter they want to be helpful. The problem comes when the friendliness leads to information being shared that is not ready to be shared or not part of the story.

This comes from a need to "help out" the reporter. I see it with business people who feel the press should help bolster the community by not covering bad news and only covering good news (kind of the way the Soviet Union handled press relations). The reporter is there to get a story, not to support the community, not to help you get the word out, and not to make the future better.

After information is out, the person who released the info will say, "I just wanted to help out the reporter." Even worse I see people desperately trying to be friends with a reporter so they give more information than they should, hoping the information will ingratiate them in some way. Usually, such mistakes become a real problem with coworkers or damaging to the organization.

My advice is to be friendly, but not friends with reporters. They have an important job to do. In a way, they are like mandatory reporters of abuse; reporters are mandatory reporters of interesting stories. Don't fall in the trap.

The second real mistake is *arrogance*. I have a little story to tell that is a wonderful example of how arrogance gets in the way of good press work. My wife is a television reporter. A prominent hospital administrator called her after a newscast. He announced to her that he was now grading all stories about his organization and that the last story got a "C." My wife's response was typical of any working journalist; she wanted to know how she could get an "F."

The real problem is that the administrator was treating the press as if they were pupils he had to educate. It is true that some education does need to take place with reporters, but the arrogance of his manner and thought did nothing for his hospital. It puffed up his ego and probably gave him something to tell his cronies over a cocktail, but the net effect was detrimental to the hospital.

Arrogance can show itself in other ways. I've heard many people say "I'm good with the press, I'll just wing it." CEOs especially tend to think this way. It is funny because these same CEOs will spend hours and many dollars trying to perfect a golf shot, but not a minute practicing for a press interview. I've seen people try to bully reporters in one way or another. What is funny is that, eventually the press wins. They always have the last word.

Deposition vs Interview

As a young executive at a television station, I was given the "wonderful opportunity" of helping to fire someone. Eventually, this action led to a lawsuit and my first experience with a deposition. As I prepared for the meeting with the opposing counsel, it struck me that this experience is no different than preparing for an interview with a reporter.

In a deposition, your answer is being written down word-for-word by a court reporter. Anything you say in the deposition can be used against you in a court of law in the future. The deposition is probably the most important part of a court case. The same is true for an interview with the press. What you say is being recorded and it can be used against you not in the courtroom, but in the court of public opinion.

The advice I was being given by a $300-an-hour attorney is perfect preparation for an interview with the press. The two-day intensive session and role playing can be boiled down to three nuggets:

- Answer truthfully.
- Only answer the question asked—don't offer information.
- Pause before you speak.

A lot of people think that PR is spinning or telling lies. That could not be farther from the truth. For my clients I say, the truth is all you can tell. Now, there may be areas you can't speak about, but what you can say must be true, or don't say it. Reporters, especially television reporters, have an uncanny knack of being able to spot a lie. It probably comes from watching tapes of so many interviews. If you've ever watched people being interviewed, it is amazing how a lie comes through the screen. So don't rely on your acting skills, just tell the truth.

The second lesson from depositions is: Only answer the question asked. Don't offer other information. It is the reporter's job to ask questions. Your job is to answer. But there is no need to make the job easy for the reporter, especially if the story is a sticky issue for your organization. Don't offer extraneous information, it can only get you into trouble. Just keep to the facts.

And then there is the final area—pausing. Pausing is the most important PR skill you will learn from this book. If you don't remember anything else, remember pausing. This is another technique we will talk about later, called flagging. Pausing is a simple technique that can save you in an interview. The technique is simply this: You are asked a question, you pause, think about the question and your answer, and then answer. The pause, no matter how long will not be reported. In video the editor will just go to when you first start talking. In print, it won't be included because it is not part of the story. Imagine a reporter writing, ". . . after a long pause the person said . . . ." It just won't happen. The reporter wants the meat, they won't leave the bun in the copy.

How does pausing help? Simple, it avoids the "Ummms" and "Ahhhhs" people naturally put in speech. Listen to how people answer your questions: Do they sometimes start talking even before the entire question is out of your mouth? If they do, then such persons will not make good spokespeople for your organization. You need to carefully listen to the question, pause, and then decide what you are going to say. Then say it in a nice sound bite—not some long-winded rambling diatribe filled with "like," "um" and "ah."

Judo Journalism

An interview is like judo. You face off with your opponent studying each other's moves. Until, whamo! You find yourself flat on your back. In judo you use the opponent's weight against them. In judo journalism you use the opponent's weight—a journalist's weight is time-pressure—to your advantage.

Reporters are under incredible time-pressure. Broadcast journalists have hard deadlines throughout the day; print journalists have one hard deadline to meet each day. Only cooks know the kind of environment journalists work in. This pressure usually makes journalists demanding. The deadline looms, so they must be pushy to get the story to bed. When a journalist calls and says they need an answer right away before deadline, believe them. If you don't respond, the story will run without your side of the story represented. But, you can use this time pressure to your advantage as well. For example, when the reporter calls, ask when the deadline for the story is. That way you now know when you need to have your information in. Then simply say, "I don't have the answer to that but I'll get back to you in an hour." This gives you time to pull together your thoughts, do a little research and then come back to the reporter fully prepped with a sound, tight answer. If you don't know the answer, help the journalist out, "I don't know the answer to that, but you know who does is _____. When you find the answer to that please call me back." Then make sure you call the person you referred to before the journalist has a chance to make the call.

A judo-journalist move to watch for is what we call the "leg sweep." The reporter uses a series of simple 'yes' questions to lull you into letting down your guard and then the big-whammy question. If you find yourself saying yes to a lot of simple questions, be on your guard. This technique is also used when the reporter asks you several personal questions at the beginning of the interview to make you feel at ease, and then blamo, you're on your heels heading toward the mat with your organization close behind. The leg sweep: using a series of simple yes questions to move you toward the big-whammy question.

The next technique is called the "flip" or "hooking." In our conversational nature we feel the need to end thoughts with throw-away lines such as "That's why we are a safe organization. Most of the time we do a good job." The attentive reporter will take the last part of your thought and flip it into a cheap question: "Only most of the time? What happens during the other times?" Or, you might end a sentence with, "That's just one of the reasons." "Oh, what are the other reasons?" By hooking onto the end of your sentence the reporter seems to be able to continue questioning when you are really done with that topic. How to avoid it? End your thought and stop talking. The little run-on thoughts are fine talking to your friends, but to a reporter they can become deadly.

Another simple judo move is to block an attack. This is to be used when a hostile or hypothetical question is thrown your way. For example, if an employee did something at your organization that warranted coverage (a police action) and the reporter asked you about the person. You would block that question with, "It is our policy not to discuss personnel issues, but what I can tell you is this . . ." Then go on and answer what you want. Another block is "I think what you're really asking is . . ." or, "that speaks to a bigger issue and that is . . ." In other words, you are blocking the question you can't answer, and you are offering information that could be quoted. Blocking allows you to answer the question quickly, and then use a transition to bridge to your message. "That's a good point, but what is important to remember is . . ." "Let me put that into perspective . . . or "Our research shows . . ." Remember, as in judo, the interview is a fluid dance back and forth. You can parry any advance and turn it to your advantage with a few simple techniques.

Remember that the reporter is looking for the "media moment," when you let your guard down and your emotions show. Now, it is good to show your passion, but you have information to share. Reporters, especially television reporters, are looking for the emotion.

So how do you let the reporter know what is important, or when to let passion show through? The technique is called "Flagging." I did a flag when I talked about pausing: *Pausing is the most important PR skill you will learn from this book. If you don't remember anything else, remember pausing.* This technique helps the reporter find the great sound bite or good quote. I've seen PR "black-belts" actually point at the reporter's notebook and tell the reporter to make sure he or she writes the statement down because it is so important. Some other good flags are: "You must remember this . . . ," The main point to remember is . . ." But don't use this overused cliché: "At the end of day . . ."

Some people even go as far as counting down the top issues. For example, I have three points to make . . . and then the person lists them. This counting down technique is effective, but make sure you remember all the points you wanted to make.

Never Let a Mistake Go Unchallenged

Reporters are human, and they do make mistakes. When you hear an inaccuracy in the questions or comments of a reporter, you must stop the interview and correct the mistake. You cannot afford to have misinformation make it into the paper or television story. Once it is in, no retraction can correct it. This is an issue because many times reporters will pull old stories when they are writing a new one about your organization. If the information is wrong it will continue to follow you until it is corrected in the file copy. How you handle it is important. You need to be friendly, but firm in order to make sure you have applied enough emphasis to make sure the infraction is not repeated or worse, placed in the story.

However, your mistakes are another issue altogether. If you or your organization has made a mistake and there is person who has been wronged; don't apologize to the world for your error. Apologize to the person you offended. Apologize to that person privately. Publicly state how you'll make the future better, but there is no reason to apologize to everyone for your error. Keep positive, stay forward-looking and remind people how your past has been stellar and the future now looks much brighter.

If You're Going Off the Record You're Off Your Rocker

Why do people feel they must tell things to reporters? Reporters survive on this need to blab. And the good reporters are excellent listeners. I watch people with my wife who is a television anchor/reporter. They tell her everything. The best are the people who begin with, "I probably shouldn't tell you this, but . . . yada, yada, yada." People talk and talk until they are blue in the face, telling every secret, nuance or detail of their business.

What amazes me most is that some believe that the simple phrase "this is off the record" gives the person some protection. There is no reporter-interviewee protection; you are not talking to a journalist-priest. You're talking to a person who gets paid to tell other people things: lots and lots of other people. Yes, some will abide by the "off the record" promise. But why do you feel the need to take the chance? What can you really gain? You can only cause serious issues for yourself, your organization or your board of directors.

You have to be off your rocker to be off the record. Another ploy that is used by reporters is to call an exchange "deep background." If you think you're safe giving deep background then you're in deep _____.

When I give speeches on media training I usually ask how many people in the audience have trained to be interviewed. Usually there are one to two people. I then hold up *The Reporter's Handbook* written by Steve Weinberg and tell the audiences, "Here's an entire book written on how to be a reporter." Reporters are trained and experienced at getting people on the record. They do it everyday. Most reporters also went to school to learn these techniques, but you probably didn't take a class on being interviewed. Here is what one of the textbooks says about "off the record" instances. This is from *The Report's Handbook*:

"If the investigator expects the interview to be on the record but the source invokes off-the-record background or some other unacceptable condition during the session, there are countermoves. One possibility is to listen respectfully, then later interject 'that information you shared earlier is fascinating. Is there any way I can quote you about that?' Another possibility is to find out from the source whether documents or other persons might reveal the same information. An investigator can stand on principle, telling the source that everything must be on the record because that was the original verbal or implied contract. Standing on principal is easier for an investigator if there is no prior relationship with the source and if there is little likelihood of such a relationship developing in the future."

Did you pick up on the fact that off the record is an 'unacceptable' response? It is unacceptable for the reporter and for us as PR professionals.

Do you remember when Connie Chung interviewed Newt Gingrich's mom? After the interview was officially over, Mrs. Chung leaned over and asked, "Just between you and me what do you really think about Hillary Clinton?" And Mrs. Gingrich told her exactly what she thought. We'll it wasn't between "you and me" it was being recorded the entire time. Was it ethically wrong? I don't know, and don't care. Most people were mad at Connie Chung. I'm sorry, that is stupid. Why did Mrs. Gingrich feel the need to share with Connie Chung? Mrs. Chung is a reporter paid to get the inside story. Mrs. Gingrich is a blabber, and in some ways a liar, because what she said in the interview is not what she said after the interview. What was she thinking? People say, ". . . well, she was older." So experience means nothing? Mrs. Gingrich was a public figure and the reason they wanted to interview her was because she might say something juicy. For some unknown reason, people like to blab to reporters. The reporters are ready, you are probably not.

Another little issue is the "No Comment" fallback. The problem with "no comment" is that the television show 60 Minutes inadvertently redefined the phrase to mean "I'm guilty." You can always comment. Undoubtedly someone from the other side of the story will comment—or worse someone from a competing organization will comment.

Now, I'm not naïve: there are many issues that you cannot comment on, but you can always make a comment. Let's set a scenario: Money has been embezzled from your organization, the person has been arrested (so it is public knowledge) and a reporter from the local television station has called you. Your first inclination is that you cannot speak about employee matters or anything about the investigation. So, you would say "no comment?" Wrong-o! That means all the reported comment is going to come from court documents, the police and the prosecuting attorney. Will they speak well of your organization? Not a chance. So, what do you say? Well if the reporter ends his two-minute story with a standup in front of your building and says "and we contacted United Way and they had no comment." You look like you're not doing anything. Your attorney will be happy; she works in the court of law. Your stakeholders will not be happy: they live in the court of public opinion. So, I would recommend talking to the reporter, however make sure you are prepared and disciplined in your response. Here is the simple way to handle the interview: Don't answer the questions the reporter asks, say what you want people to know. For example: *"Bob you know I can't comment on specific employee issues, but what I can tell you is that we at United Way are cooperating with the police in any and every way; we are conducting our own thorough investigation into this matter, and we've hired an accounting firm to immediately take charge of our finances and change any accounting practices that seem suspect so that people can have renewed confidence in our organization."* You've shown the community that you are addressing this issue head on, you've taken action, and you have given people a sense that going forward all will be okay. So a good follow-up question from the reporter would be "so you admit there was an embezzlement?" *"Bob, you know I can't speak about the ongoing investigation, but I can tell you is that Blank and Blank Accounting firm is putting into place accounting practices better than the industry standard."* And, then the smart reporter will ask, "Why didn't you have those practices in before the embezzlement?" *"Bob I can't speak about an ongoing investigation, but what I can say is that United Way is committed to serving the people of this community and we are doing everything in our power to bring the best accounting practices into play."* Now imagine that one little 20-second sound bite is used, which one do you think the press would use? Any one of these would be better than "no comment."

Don't try this at a press conference. That may seem a convenient way to get it all over at once, but one-on-one will be much more effective. It is easier to mentally spar with one person than a room full of trained reporters.

These techniques work best with real journalists. Blogger-reporters will change things—especially with the speed of reporting and the amount of editorializing in stories—but it will take time to see if the blogger world really becomes a local market voice.

The Sound Bites

I attended a League of Women Voters forum for a local state senate race. I was there for a mission-driven organization hoping to ask questions about child welfare funding. The forum was packed with people. I had never been to a forum like this and I was excited to see the political process and the debate first hand. I was shocked at the how the League had decided to conduct the debate. First the moderator would edit the questions which didn't sound like a debate or democracy; and second, the candidates would be given 30 seconds to respond to each question. Thirty seconds? That is the length of a commercial. It is a sound bite. Even at this public debate, the politicians were limited to sound bites. Then I realized, it is not the press that likes sound bites, it is everyone.

So, the press uses sound bites. It is time to quit complaining about sound bites and begin a process of using sound bites to your advantage. If you're going to be a successful speaker then you need to learn to speak in sound bites. Don't add conjunctions. One of the best ways to do this is to break your statements into poignant, bite-sized nuggets. Don't add conjunctions. Learn to put a period at the end of a thought, and pause. For most, the end of the sentence is where the quote falls apart.

One question

Many times a reporter will ask two questions at once, especially at press conferences. Because there is enough going on at the time, just answer one question at a time. Pick the question you want to answer and only answer that question. You will want to repeat the question (giving you time to think) and pause (giving you more time) and then answer the question. If the reporter is not happy with the answer he will ask the other question. This is not a dodge, it is simplifying the interview situation so that you don't get confused trying to remember questions when you should focus all you efforts on answers.

Super _____ Syndrome

The saddest part of PR is watching people self-destruct in an interview. And you see it all the time. I call it the Super "fill in the blank" Syndrome. This seems to be a lesson taught at law schools and medical schools all across the country because you can fill the blank with "lawyer" or "doctor" with ease.

In your office you see the person assume control: "I know someone in the press I'll call them and explain the situation," or, "I was good at debate, I'll talk to the press." It's not a debate, but it can be a slaughter. When the reporter gets back to the office he or she will write the story. The Super Syndrome ends as the reporter thinks "what a jerk" and then writes the story.

Here is what happens: The press calls, and the Super Lawyer declares that he can handle the press. Since he is super he doesn't prepare for the encounter because he is a trained debater. Unfortunately, in the court of public opinion you cannot strike anything from the record, there is no judge presiding to keep things orderly and there is no objection or sidebar opportunity. The worst example of this was a private jet firm that was going out of business. My firm was sort-of hired to handle the negative PR that was about to descend on the firm as it declared bankruptcy. Unfortunately, the lawyer on the case canceled our services. When reporters went to the airport to do the story, they were not greeted with any respect. After the lawyer dodged every question with "no comment," one frustrated reporter asked, "When will you be making a statement." The lawyer yelled back, "not now, not ever." I didn't add all the exclamation points that the statement deserved—but try running a business after that. You are guaranteed that no stories will run after that, especially any 'positive' stories. For the record, the private jet service was never heard from again.

What are ways to avoid the Super Syndrome?

- Be prepared. Even if you have been to the toughest law school in America, try this little trick: Write your three main messages on a 3 X 5 inch card. You can set it on your desk or hold it. The reporter is not going to report that you referred to notes as you answered questions or the television reporter is not going to show you looking at your notes in the story because there is not time. It is a simple PR tool that works. The reporter has a notebook with questions and they will come prepared to ask questions, you need to prepare to answer. Even in a live situation, hold the card. If you get caught you can refer to the card. A look down at your notes looks a lot better than stumbling for an answer.

- Reporters are people. Don't assume journalists are not real people. They are as human as you are and they have feelings. If you are rude to the reporter, don't expect that rudeness to be unrewarded in the story. Reporters try to separate themselves from the situations, but they are not machines. Their emotions will have an impact on the story. Make sure you are not the cause of that by thinking you are smarter, more quick-thinking or better than reporters. Those thoughts will come through in your quotes and will especially shine on the camera.

- Return reporters calls. Reporters are on deadline. If you don't return the call promptly you will miss the opportunity. Most stories air the day of the call or the next day. So make sure you are available.

- Know deadlines. Ask the reporter right away what the deadline is for the story. Also find out general deadlines for stories. Morning and afternoon papers have different deadlines; television news organizations have deadlines throughout the day. If you are trying to have a television station do a live shot, you need to have your event or announcement right at the top of a newscast. Then you must make sure something is happening at that time.

- Respect dates. Newsrooms are just like any business: People take days off, people get sick, people take long weekends. Reporters have lives outside of the newsroom and you need to understand how your story may be impacted by the calendar. If you hold your open house on Memorial Day Saturday there may only be one or two reporters at the TV station to cover all the news. If a fire starts or some other event happens that is larger there is a good chance your event will not be covered.

Just the Facts

When preparing for your interview, prepare a fact sheet to give to the reporter. It will help the reporter when they get back to the newsroom and begin to write the story. The fact-sheet should be bulleted information about the story, but it also should give some of the general information about your organization: date opened, number of people served, annual budget, number of employees, etc. Have you ever come back from a seminar and not been able to read your writing? That's why a fact-sheet can be so helpful and make sure that the facts are right in the story.

A lot of people complain that they are misquoted. But what happens the most is that the person talks so fast or never stops talking that it is impossible for the reporter to keep up. Watch your speed as you talk. Wait until the reporter has finished writing to begin another quote. Even though reporters are fast note-takers and typists they can only go so fast. Repeating a good quote will help the reporter make sure they have it right and you might say it better the second time. This is especially a good practice for television. Most reporters I've talked with do not want to misquote anybody; it is just part of the human process of communication. The other interesting fact I've observed is that people will say they are misquoted even when they are recorded on tape. If you want to really know what you said, don't rely on your memory; record your session so you can hear exactly how you stated the answer. You will be amazed at how accurate reporters usually are.

The Press Are People Too

I know we have talked about this a bit, but you must be friendly no matter what the topic or your schedule. There is nothing worse than the daily grind of deadlines in a newsroom. You need to respect this pressure and understand it. The reporter may be rude. Remember that they have probably been lied to, used, and abused so they are skeptical, maybe even cynical. Their attitude is well-earned. In spite of this, you need to treat the reporters with respect. Don't confuse this with being friends of reporters, just be friendly. You want the best possible story to run so please don't let your ego get in the way of the press coverage.

Another way to gain the respect of reporters is to call when you have a story idea that does not personally help you or your organization, but does help the reporter. Most people call when they have a story that will benefit them in some way. Calling on these other issues will give you credibility when you call with a story about your organization.

Finally, send a thank-you note to the reporter after the story. If they did an excellent job send a note to the news director. However, don't thank the reporter for the "publicity." That will get any good journalist's underwear in a bunch. Publicity is not the reporter's job. Reporting is the job. Thank the person for a well-rounded story; thank him or her for a balanced approach to a difficult subject; thank the reporter for doing a thorough job. Just don't say "publicity."

Feed 'em Food and PR at Breakfasts

Reaching out to the community is a daunting task. How do you reach hundreds of community leaders effectively? One way is to invite them to breakfast.

Most local newspapers run an unceremonious area in the business section featuring the mugs-shots of people from the community. These announcements are for company and organization new hires and promotions, and for new board members of mission-driven organizations.

As you watch this section over the course of a year you will notice that most of these people are community leaders or up-and-coming community leaders. Many papers are also running sections featuring young community leaders. Usually, these sections are called "40 under 40" or "Women of Achievement." Any of these special recognition efforts as well as the regular "People in the News" sections are great fodder for your next PR guerrilla technique.

Begin collecting these names and once per month or once every two months, invite these people to a special breakfast at your organization in honor of their achievement. At the breakfast make sure to have a short program about your organization and a chance for the people invited to mingle and network.

The reason for the breakfast is that it guarantees to the invitees that they are not granting a major investment of their time. The morning scheduling does not usually conflict with other activities.

If you feel the need to expand your program, invite a well-known CEO from the community (hopefully one from your board) to address the group.

In fact, invite some CEOs after you read about an achievement at the company. The key is to invite people who have received some recognition. It is important to make sure you mention the achievement (and the newspaper recognition) in the invitation. This will help provide a legitimate reason for the breakfast and encourage attendance.

Don't be afraid to invite local legislators and politicians to the regular breakfasts. They will add some importance to the event and help you promote your causes as well.

It is better to hold many breakfasts of smaller numbers than to expect large crowds at one big event. This is not an event. It is "guerrilla marketing," so you should be happy when only a few attend because then you will have more time to get to know these soon to be community leaders. You also have the opportunity to improve your breakfasts as you go.

Also, don't skimp on the food or the variety. You want people buzzing about the breakfast not complaining later. Try to have one very special item at the breakfast. Serve lattes or special coffees to give people something to talk about at work after the breakfast. Have some light music playing. This will help open sleepy eyes and fill the room with noise even when there are only a few people in attendance.

Make sure you have enough staff on hand to greet each person as they walk into the room. Nothing is worse than attending an occasion even in a strange setting, not knowing anyone and then be ignored. You may want to invite the person and allow them to bring a spouse or friend to the breakfast. It may increase attendance, and certainly enhances the experience for the attendee.

Speakers Bureau

This is a joke at most organizations. It is part of almost every strategic plan, goal-setting meeting, board retreat or brainstorming session. The problem is that like any planning process, unless you have some clear goals from which to measure success, you are doomed to failure. This effort invariably gets shelved each year until someone righteously says, "We've got to get out into the community." Followed by, "How about a speakers bureau?"

A speaker's bureau will do nothing for you to get speakers into "the community." A plan of action will.

Hire a temporary employee for two days. Have the person call every service organization (Rotary, Exchange Club, Kiwanis) in your service area. Have this person start a databank that includes the name, location, date and time the group meets, program chair, and topics that the club loves to hear about. Next have your temporary employee call all the large churches in your area to see if they have meetings that require speakers.

Once you have your database built, contact all the chambers of commerce in your area. Ask (beg if you must, or if one of your board members is a chamber board member you are already on your way) if you can contact the "presidents clubs" in the area and secure a list of those groups. The chambers may also know of other groups looking for speakers.

Once you have a list mail a letter to the contacts telling them that you are available to speak to their groups and the possible topics you may cover. Be mindful if a major issue has just appeared in the paper or on television. For example, if the headline states Linn County Child Abuse Incidents Double, make sure you either include a copy of the article, or mention that you can talk about the issues and solutions to this hot topic.

Don't be disheartened if you don't get many opportunities to speak right away. Many of these groups work months in advance. And some of these groups have regular meeting topics each year (honoring high school athletes, honoring top academics in the area, state of the city address etc).

When you get the chance to speak be prepared. Work up a short PowerPoint Presentation that can be improved as you add more speaking engagements. Don't put the audience to sleep (if you speak at noon Rotaries someone will always fall asleep) with a lot of facts. Tell great, surprising stories that are easy to remember, and showcase how your organization makes a difference every day. A leave-behind such as a brochure and a small specialty item is not necessary. If you feel you must, prepare a bookmark with fast facts printed on it. They fit easily in a breast coat pocket or purse and they are less likely to be pitched right after the speech. They are also more likely to be read.

Do not ask for money. That is an amateur-hour move. If you want support from the group meet with the executive committee of the organization after you have made a presentation. Then ask for a sizeable gift.

Make PR Happen

P ublicity is not a science. It is an art. Nuance, moves on a chess board, out-thinking the press is all part of a delicate balance that requires never assuming any moves the press will make. Too many times we assume the press will just cover something because we ask.

I talked with an organization that wanted to get some publicity about a car-giveaway the organization was conducting. The day of the drawing, the organization hired a video crew for about $3,000 to make sure that it had the day documented. The hope was that the local TV stations would use the video for stories. Unfortunately, the TV stations were not interested. The newspaper was not interested. The radio stations were not interested.

The real problem was that the organization did not carefully analyze its goals. It wanted coverage. It was willing to spend $3,000 to publicize the event. What's an organization to do? The real mistake was assuming that the press was interested in a car-giveaway. There are many car-giveaways in a year, so what distinctive approach, should you use to make sure that the press cannot stay away from your story? In this case, nothing. The person had already been selected and notified and was just coming down to the organization to pick up the car.

The solution is simple: The cost of a full-page ad would have been about $3,000 for the mission-driven organization. In fact, a smaller ad could have been purchased every day for that week, featuring the winner, the organization and a little information about the organization. The ad could have been designed in such a way that it would have been more effective than a newspaper or television story.

When you're faced with a situation where your goals are clear you must make sure that the coverage occurs. The best way is to buy the space, promote the event and then seek press coverage as well. Again, knowing the true goal of your marketing can help lead to better decisions and better actions that will yield results. The video tape of the winner is still sitting on the shelf, never seen.

Logo Wall or Banner

This is the simplest trick, but very few seem to take advantage of it. Think of all the times when you had a group function, press conference or made a speech. At each of those photographs were usually taken. What was in the background of the picture? For most organizations, the answer is nothing. This is definitely a lost opportunity for some free, long-term publicity.

Next time you watch the Oscars, pay close attention to the wall behind the stars as they are interviewed and photographed behind the stage after they have won. The background wall is completely marked with the logo and name of the awards. The Oscar group knows it is in competition with a growing number of other movie award ceremonies. One way to keep the Oscar on top of its pedestal is to make sure there is no doubt that this star won an Oscar. But there is another residual effect. As the weeks go by and a magazine or newspaper needs a photo of this star, there is a chance that the publication will use the photo of the star with the Oscar background.

A simple logo will not do. You must dominate the background and make sure that at any angle there is a logo in the background. This may give your logos a wallpaper effect, but the payoff is down the road when the photo adorns a refrigerator, is used in a newsletter or is shared with others.

We have seen countless times when the Governor or some other dignitary visits an organization and the press rolls out to cover the event. When the story airs there is no mention of the organization, however a carefully placed logo-wall would have been in every shot.

You can't afford a large ad budget, so you must take every opportunity to get your logo out in front of various audiences. Another valuable place for logo identification is at the podium anytime you speak. Don't worry about the Marriott sign or Hilton sign. Place your sign on the podium for your presentation: it's like a mini-billboard, only displaying for an hour, but the audience is usually right on target. Again, the podium is where the focus of the photographer is directed as well as the audience. Rotarians have a tendency to get a little sleepy after a big lunch, so the logo reminder is especially important at those events.

We hear mission-driven PR people and CEOs complaining all the time that they did not get their name mentioned in a news report. If they had a big, bright logo behind them it wouldn't matter.

Publicity Stunts Can Be Big for Your Public Relations

Too many times, mission-driven organizations have trouble standing out in the crowd of good intentions. It seems as if the passionate advocate is lost somewhere in the day-to-day grind of running an organization. Just think of all the diseases that are clamoring for attention: American Cancer Association, the Kidney Foundation, Breast Cancer, and Juvenile Diabetes Association.

One way to stand up and stand out is to hold a special event so large that the media must cover it. The resulting talk-value gives your marketing life all its own.

The press likes to call these actions "publicity stunts." Maybe this is a good name. Remember the story about the Virgin Mary on the grilled-cheese sandwich? The woman who found it decided to sell the sacred sandwich on e-Bay. The sandwich sold for $28,000. The woman certainly was ecstatic, but the company that bought the sandwich won the "big enchilada." GoldenPalace. com paid the sum and couldn't have been happier. GoldenPalace is an online gambling site. It really doesn't have a place to display the grilled-cheesed sandwich. But, what it does have is incredible name-recognition because of the purchase. Newspapers, television stations, radio stations and magazines around the world ran the story about the $28,000 sandwich. Most probably wondered out loud why GoldenPalace.com would buy that old bread. However, the value continues. Even this mention in this book is worth some advertising value and continues to pay dividends to the company. According to *"Business 2.0,"* what the $1 million GoldenPalace.com spends on outrageous purchases is easily worth $30 million dollars in advertising.

You can't spend $28,000 on a grilled-cheese sandwich? What can you do? Start by thinking about the "talk-value" of events and opportunities.

One organization in Iowa put out a display of shoes at malls. Each pair of shoes represented a person who had died from cigarette smoking. The shoes were the perfect metaphor. The event itself drew little attention, but the advertising campaign and press coverage were powerful.

The problem is that this approach can be daunting because of the sheer size needed to impress people and the logistics to get it done. However, it is the logistical effort that makes the event so worthy of attention. Of course, the set-up is a strong visual for photographers and videographers.

Let's say you work with organ-donation and the waiting list for your state is 300 people. You've seen the events with white crosses signifying farms closings or abortions. These events don't get noticed because there are one or two crosses. I would recommend a field of 300 cut-out people standing in a row on the state Capitol's grounds. The event will take a boatload of coordination and volunteers, but it can be done and be extremely effective. If some of the volunteers are people on the list as well, it is a PR dream.

In order for this to be effective you must go over the top: the number must be surprising and visually arresting to passers-by. This brings up another important consideration, where to do the event? You must have considerable traffic for the event to be noticed. Billboard companies can give you traffic counts for specific billboard locations. Use these to plan where your event will attract the most attention even if the press does not cover you at first.

You Will Have a Crisis

"I learned there are troubles of more than one kind. Some come from
ahead and some come from behind."
Dr. Seuss

D r. Seuss understood crisis communications. In front is the issue you
are dealing with: a disgruntled employee, a law suit, a death on
the job. Behind you comes a new "trouble" called the press. Just when you
need the publicity the least, the press is nipping at your heels as you run to
control the fire of the unfolding crisis.

In the course of a few weeks, two mission-driven organizations went
from peaceful organizations to ones in major crisis-mode. One was a science
museum and the other was an organization that works with the disabled.
Both were in the throes of large capital campaigns. Both were hit by major
embezzlements of funds. In fact, the science museum had $250,000 taken
and was then $250,000 short on the capital campaign. Coincidence?

What happens next? Well the press usually calls after the embezzlement
is revealed. Board members start to ask questions, and some may decide to
run with the new board member rules. Then there are the contributors who
worry their money may have been taken, and finally there are those in the
general public who only now know your organization exists.

The point is not to address your accounting practices, although that is
not a bad idea. Instead, know that a crisis may be lurking close by, and in
fact may be festering in your organization even now.

Now that you know a crisis is going to hit your organization, there is no
excuse for not having a crisis communications plan ready to roll.

What should be in the plan?

- A call tree with contact numbers, cell phones, parent's phones, lake-home phones of all the key people in the organization
- Sample press releases to cover most of the major catastrophes that may strike your organization
- Talking points about your organization (facts and details that will be critical to answering tough questions)
- Numbers of the press and press people who understand your organization
- Web information ready to post
- An employee handbook for reference
- Your plan of attack

It used to be the "M-O" of business to lay low when a crisis would strike. When accounting scandals rocked American International Group, however, AIG used an aggressive advertising campaign to respond and begin the positive spin. "In the age of instant news and tighter financial regulation, staying silent isn't an option. These days, it seems, the best offense is a good ad," says *BusinessWeek* (July 4, 2005).

Unfortunately, in the two examples of embezzlement I gave you, the organizations chose to put their heads in the sand. The real problem is that in today's hyper-competitive marketplace, all you need is a little bad press that sends people to other organizations: volunteers, contributors, potential board members, and potential employees. You can't stop the crisis from happening, but how you handle the situation will be critical to your short-term (and in some cases long-term) growth.

There is a Market

As I sat and talked with the director of the Meals on Wheels service in Cedar Rapids I was struck by the power of a strong mission. Unlike profit companies, the *true* mission is not always so obvious. What also struck me was the potential of the Meals on Wheels program for all seniors: It is a service that will deliver a hot meal to seniors and check on them each week or every day.

The marketer in me saw a huge potential for the kids who are trying to take care of distant parents. My brain said, "Could we better deliver our mission if we could expand this program to help all seniors?" I know there is so much to think about in connection with this, but as Donald Trump has said, "If you're going to be thinking anyway, why not think big."

Marketing is so much more than ads and brochures. It is about your strategy. It is time for mission-driven organizations to look skyward, build momentum, make some money, and deliver on mission (now and in the future).

I'm sure many of the ideas seem a bit strange, far fetched, and untenable in the "nonprofit" world. But there is a shift-change coming.

In David Shenk's book *Data Smog*, he said that in 1970 we were exposed to more than 550 messages a day. Now that number is 3,000 messages. We must not only break out of the "nonprofit" clutter, but we must also compete in the profit clutter. How do you become relevant? That is a key question and one you and your board will need to wrestle with in your strategic planning meetings.

Marketing is Holistic

My hope is that after reading this book and all the short chapters, you will see how the puzzle fits together. Marketing is not ads, brochures and signs—it is all of those. In medicine, the combination of all approaches is called a holistic approach to healthcare, looking at every aspect of the patient to help move toward better health.

You must look at your organization from the target audience's point-of-view and then analyze how that audience *experiences* your organization.

I spoke to a Management Development Institute of the National Home Furniture Association in High Point, North Carolina. We did a little experiment. We took all the furniture ads from one weekend in a local paper and then photographed them all together. We then cut out ads from *Vanity Fair* and photographed them as well. The dramatic difference was apparent to all in the room. One photo was of an industry trying to yell at an audience. Most of those ads were probably designed by men. The second group of ads from *Vanity Fair* was connecting with an audience. The ads looked like women designed the ads to communicate with women. In the first group, there was copy listing everything for sale, photos of a few pieces of furniture and bold headlines such as Everything Must Go, We Must Reduce Inventory, Lost Our Lease, and Our Biggest Sale Ever. In the *Vanity Fair* ads, the focus was on the audience. There were humanized ads that told a story, the benefits of products, children in some ads, and forward-sounding copy. Women buy most of the furniture, but few ads really take that into account.

Holistic marketing centers on the target audience and works out from there. If you are making a brochure for fundraising, your audience will be much different than a general informational brochure for the local Rotary clubs. Narrow your focus and it will expand your communications horizons.

The End of the Book
Beginning of Your Marketing Effort

www.ingramcontent.com/pod-product-compliance
Lightning Source LLC
Chambersburg PA
CBHW030006190526
45157CB00014B/556